Faculty Guide

for

Allyn and Bacon
Mind Matters

ISBN 0-205-32214-X

Printed in the United States of America

10 9 8 7 6 5 4 3 2   03 02 01 00

Faculty Guide

for

Allyn and Bacon
Mind Matters

James Hilton
University of Michigan

Charles Perdue
West Virginia State College

Allyn and Bacon
Boston   London   Toronto   Sydney   Tokyo   Singapore

Table of Contents

AUTHORS' WELCOME

As the authors of the **Allyn and Bacon Mind Matters** CD-ROM, we would like to take this opportunity to welcome you and tell you a little bit about it. Four years ago we were watching James Hilton's son play on the computer. At the time, Michael Hilton was 5 years old and, although he could not yet read, we were amazed at the fact that he had no trouble playing on the computer. As we watched, we also began to realize that he was "learning" an awful lot while playing. More importantly, he was learning with a joy and enthusiasm that is too rarely achieved in the classroom. From that moment, we were hooked. We became obsessed with the idea of finding ways to use digital technology to enhance the teaching and learning of psychology. We looked at every piece of software we could find. We bought all kinds of CD-ROMs, from digital cookbooks to computer games. We drove the people around us nuts. Fortunately, just as the patience of those we love began to wear thin, we convinced Allyn and Bacon (then AWL) to join us in the quest to use digital technology to make psychology more engaging, interactive, informative, and fun.

With their support, we designed a prototype that consisted of a series of computerized learning activities. The prototype was then submitted to a semester's worth of testing in actual classrooms. We learned a great deal. For example, we learned that some of the things that work in print don't work in digital form. We learned how important it is to provide context for all of the activities. Most importantly, we learned that it's critical to get reviews and feedback at every stage of development. We then began working on this CD-ROM. Our strategy was to keep the things that worked, replace the things that didn't, and have everything reviewed for content and look and feel. We're happy with the result and hope you and your students will find it useful and enjoyable.

WHAT IS THE ALLYN AND BACON MIND MATTERS CD?

The CD-ROM is designed to work as a supplement to virtually any introductory psychology textbook. It includes chapters devoted to history, methods, biopsychology, learning, memory, sensation, and perception. Each chapter, in turn, contains a series of self-contained modules that cover "core" psychological concepts (e.g., selective attention, signal detection theory, classical conditioning, and natural selection) through a combination of text, graphics, humor, and activities. The point was not to create an exhaustive reference tool about psychology, but rather to present and integrate concepts in ways that invite readers to explore the "science of the mind." Rather than rewarding memorization, the CD-ROM is designed to nurture exploration and integration.

WHAT KINDS OF ACTIVITIES ARE ON THE DISK?

The CD-ROM includes a variety of activities ranging from movies and interactive animations to full-blown simulations and interactive explorations. Every chapter includes interactive quizzes, rapid reviews, movies and sounds. But every chapter also includes a more ambitious set of activities that allow students to experience abstract principles and theories concretely. Because we think this is the most exciting and novel aspect of the **Allyn and Bacon Mind Matters** CD-

ROM we've provide thumbnail descriptions of six of these activities to give you a feel for what they are like. More complete descriptions of these and all the other activities are contained in the annotated guide that follows.

- **Signal Detection:** This interaction is designed to get students to see that perceptual discriminations are judgments that are influenced by both the actual stimulus information present and the person's decision criteria (their "willingness" to say that they detect something). Students are presented with a detection task (e.g., to see a true blip on a simulated "noisy" radar screen) with a stimulus that varies in its detectability. On some trials the students will be encouraged to be especially vigilant because a failure to detect the event could be disastrous (e.g., they are looking for incoming missiles, or planes in the landing pattern). On other trials, they are told that they may relax and be less vigilant. After multiple trials, students will see a table for each condition that will show their "score" in terms of hits, correct rejections, false alarms, and misses. In conjunction with relevant narration, students should see from these tables that the differing instructions influenced primarily their willingness to say that an event happened (i.e., overall accuracy remains constant, but the ratio of false alarms and misses changes).

- **Natural Selection:** In this activity, Darwin's concept of natural selection is introduced via a simulation. Students see a gaggle of simulated creatures milling about randomly on the edge of a cliff with some periodically falling off the cliff. The students can control the height of the cliff (i.e., the selection pressure) and the time frame (i.e., present, near future, and distant future). The primary goal of the simulation is to help students to see that selection is not an "intelligent" or anthropomorphic process. The simulation should help students to see that natural selection pressures can vary and thus produce effects on behavior to varying degrees. It should also help them see how adaptation occurs over generations rather than within a single generation.

- **Universality of Emotions:** In this activity, emotion is viewed from an adaptive perspective. The core concept that is presented is the notion that we have and express certain "feelings" because it is instinctive to do so. As a demonstration of the universality of several core emotions, students can play a drag and drop matching game in which they look at pictures of people expressing different emotions (from Paul Ekman's research) and match the pictures with the right emotion label.

- **The Navigable Brain:** In this activity, students can explore the functions of various parts of the brain. When students click on a particular part of the brain, they hear a brief explanation of the primary function of that area accompanied by an animation. The goal of this activity is to help students to remember both the location and primary functions of the major structures in the brain.

- **Brain Structure and Function Game:** This "drag and drop" activity requires students to match brain structures with their respective functions. Icons representing various functions (e.g. "relaying sensory data") have to be matched correctly to the corresponding structure in the brain (e.g., the thalamus). This activity should help reinforce the ideas of specialization and localization of function in the brain.

4

- **Color and Motion Afterimage:** These activities use color and motion afterimages to introduce students to the idea that visual information is processed both in the visual cortex and in the retina. The activities begin with brief explanations of the processes (i.e., receptor depletion and opponent processes) that are involved in the production of color and motion afterimage effects. The students are then given 20 seconds to adapt to either a color or motion afterimage stimulus. Following the adaptation phase, this stimulus is replaced by a colorless screen (in the case of color afterimage) or a stationary object (in the case of motion afterimage), and the students should experience an afterimage effect. (Be advised, however, that motion afterimages are extremely transient, lasting for perhaps a second or so.)

HOW CAN I USE THE PROGRAM IN MY COURSE?

The modular nature of the CD-ROM allows it to be used in a variety of ways.

- Because each concept is presented in a self-contained manner, you can use it to whet your students' appetites for topics you haven't covered yet. You could, for example, ask your class to go through the entire Sensation unit on the disk before you cover sensation in class. The activities are designed to stimulate their interest in the topic.

- Similarly, the modular nature of the CD-ROM means that your students can use it as a review tool. In keeping with this use, each chapter includes quizzes and rapid reviews. In addition, the level of writing is intended to provide summaries of the important points.

- The navigation of the disk allows you to access individual activities and use them in your lectures. The annotated guide contains suggestions for activities that are particularly well suited to this use (e.g., afterimages).

- The CD-ROM can also be used in a laboratory setting. Students can be asked to keep notes about their experiences with various activities and these notes can become the basis for class discussions, term papers, or multi-media assignments. Each chapter also includes a quiz with the option to print the results. These quizzes can be use to mark your students' progress as they work their way through the disk.

CAN I TEST STUDENTS ON THE MATERIAL COVERED ON THE DISK?

Yes. As noted above, each chapter has an interactive quiz with printable results. In addition, this guide contains additional quizzes that you can use to assess your students' progress.

HOW TECHNOLOGICALLY LITERATE MUST MY STUDENTS BE TO USE THE DISK?

Minimally. The CD-ROM is designed to be easy to use and easy to navigate. The navigation and activities are all "point and click."

HOW TECHNOLOGICALLY LITERATE MUST I BE TO USE THE CD?

If you use the CD-ROM in your lectures, you will need to know how to connect your computer to a data projector. Otherwise, you don't need to know much about the technology to use the CD-ROM. We've even included a guide below that describes each interaction and has suggestions for how to use the activities.

WHAT ELSE IS IN THIS GUIDE?

- Extensive outlines of the contents of the CD-ROM annotated with suggested web links, learning objectives, and tips on using the activities. * Due to the dynamic nature of the web, we cannot guarantee the integrity of the suggested sites .

- Photocopy ready versions of the quizzes and matching game activities that appear on the disk, plus two additional quizzes for each unit.

- Content guides linking the contents of the CD-ROM with seven leading textbooks from Allyn and Bacon.

CORRELATION GUIDES

BARON, *PSYCHOLOGY*, FIFTH EDITION

HISTORY AND METHODS

Hilton/Perdue Allyn & Bacon Mind Matters CD	Baron Psychology 5E
Psychology's Roots	Modern Psychology: What It Is and How It Originated, Ch. 1, pg. 5
Recent Trends in Psychology	Psychology 2000: Trends for the New Millennium., Ch. 1, pg. 12
The Science of Psychology	Psychology and the Scientific Method, Ch. 1, pg. 19 The Scientific Method: Its Basic Nature, Ch. 1, pg. 19 Research Methods in Psychology: How Psychologists Answer Questions About Behavior, Ch. 1, pg. 24 Extrasensory Perception: Perception without Sensation?, Ch. 3, pg. 123

BIOPSYCHOLOGY

Hilton/Perdue Allyn and Bacon Mind Matters CD	Baron Psychology 5E
Evolution and Behavior	Heredity and Behavior: Genetics and Evolutionary Psychology, Ch. 2, pg. 72 Psychology 2000: Trends for the New Millennium Psychology and Diversity: The Multicultural Perspective, Ch. 1, pg. 13 From Gender Identity to Sex-Category Constancy: How Children Come to Understand That They Are a Man or Woman, Ch. 8, pg. 321
Physiological Psychology: Neurons and the Endocrine System	Neurons: Building Blocks of the Nervous System, Ch. 2, pg. 44 The Nervous System: Its Basic Structure and Functions, Ch. 2, pg. 50 The Endocrine System: Chemical Regulators of Bodily Processes, Ch. 2, pg. 52
Physiological Psychology: The Brain	The Brain: Where Consciousness...Is, Ch. 2, pg. 55

	The Cerebral Cortex: The Core of Complex Thought, Ch. 2, pg. 58 Two Minds in One Body? Our Divided Brains, Ch. 2, pg. 61

SENSATION

Hilton/Perdue Allyn and Bacon Mind Matters CD	Baron Psychology 5E
Introduction to Sensation	Sensation and Perception: Making Contact with the World Around Us, Ch. 3, pg. 83
Sensory Transduction	Sensation: The Raw Materials of Understanding—Sensory Thresholds: How Much Stimulation is Enough?, Ch. 3, pg. 86 Vision, Ch. 3, pg. 91 The Eye: Its Basic Structure, Ch. 3, pg. 91 Hearing, Ch. 3, pg. 98 The Ear: Its Basic Structure, Ch. 3, pg. 98 Smell and Taste: The Chemical Senses, Ch. 3, pg. 106
Sensory Coding	Vision, Ch. 3, pg. 91 Color Vision, Ch. 3, pg. 96 Vision and the Brain: Processing Visual Information, Ch. 3, pg. 97 Hearing, Ch. 3, pg. 98 Pitch Perception, Ch. 3, pg. 100
Sensory Adaptation	Sensation: The Raw Materials of Understanding Ch. 3, pg. 85 Sensory Adaptation: "It Feels Great Once You Get Used to It," Ch. 3, pg. 90

PERCEPTION

Hilton/Perdue Allyn and Bacon Mind Matters CD	Baron Psychology 5E
Introduction to Perception	Perception: Putting It All Together, Ch. 3, pg. 112
Perceptual Constancy	Perception: Putting It All Together Constancies and Illusions: When Perception Succeeds–and Fails, Ch. 3, pg. 114
Perceptions as Decisions	Sensation: The Raw Materials of Understanding Sensory Thresholds: How Much stimulation is Enough?, Ch. 3, pg. 86

	Perception: Putting It All Together Some Key Perceptual Processes: Pattern and Distance, Ch. 3, pg. 118
Perceptual Illusions	Perception: Putting It All Together Constancies and Illusions: When Perception Succeeds-and Fails, Ch. 3, pg. 114

LEARNING AND MEMORY

Hilton/Perdue **Allyn and Bacon Mind Matters CD**	Baron **Psychology 5E**
Learning Through Association: Classical Conditioning	Classical Conditioning: Learning That Some Stimuli Signal Others, Ch. 5, pg. 169
Learning From Consequences: Operant Conditioning	Operant Conditioning: Learning Based on Consequences, Ch. 5, pg. 182 Research Methods: How Psychologists Study Applications of Operant Conditioning, Ch. 5, pg. 197
Opening the Black Box: Cognitive Learning	Observational Learning: Learning from the Behavior and Outcomes of Others, Ch. 5, pg. 200 Thinking: Forming Concepts and Reasoning to Conclusions, Ch. 7, pg. 249
The Process of Remembering	Human Memory: Two Influential Views, Ch. 6, pg. 210 Kinds of Information Stored in Memory, Ch. 6, pg. 214 Memory Distortion and Memory Construction, Ch. 6, pg. 226

KOSSLYN/ROSENBERG *PSYCHOLOGY: THE BRAIN, THE PERSON, THE WORLD*

HISTORY AND METHODS

Hilton/Perdue **Allyn and Bacon Mind Matters CD**	Kosslyn/Rosenberg **Psychology: The Brain, The Person, The World**
Psychology's Roots	**Psychological Science: Getting to Know You**--What Is Psychology? Ch. 1, pg. 8 **Psychology Then and Now**--The Evolution of a Science, Ch. 1, pg. 13
Recent Trends in Psychology	**Psychology Then and Now**--The Evolution of a Science, Ch. 1, pg. 13 The Psychological Way: What Today's

	Psychologists Do, Ch. 1, pg. 20
The Science of Psychology	**The Science of Psychology: Designed to Be Valid**--The Scientific Method, Ch. 1, pg. 26 The Psychologist's Toolbox: Methods for Scientific Research, Ch. 1, pg. 28 Be a Critical Consumer of Psychology, Ch. 1, pg. 33 **Sensing in Other Ways**--Extrasensory Perception (ESP), Ch. 3, pg. 124

BIOPSYCHOLOGY

Hilton/Perdue **Allyn and Bacon Mind Matters CD**	Kosslyn/Rosenberg **Psychology: The Brain, The Person, The World**
Evolution and Behavior	**Genes, Brain, and Environment: The Brain in the World**—Evolution and the Brain: The Best of All Possible Brains? Ch. 2, pg. 82 **Emotion: I Feel, Therefore I Am**—Types of Emotions: What Can You Feel? Ch. 9, pg. 312 **Interaction with People: Social Behavior**—Relationships: Having a Date, Having a Partner, Ch. 15, pg. 572 Helping Behavior: Helping Others, Ch. 15, pg. 586
Physiological Psychology: Neurons and the Endocrine System	**Brain Circuits: Making Connections**—The Neuron: A Powerful Computer, Ch. 2, pg. 46 Neurotransmitters and Neuromodulators: Bridging the Gap, Ch. 2, pg. 50 Unbalanced Brain: Coping with Bad Chemicals, Ch. 2, pg. 51 **Structure and Function: An Orchestra with many Members**—The Neuroendocrine System: It's Hormonal, Ch. 2, pg. 68
Physiological Psychology: The Brain	**Structure and Function: An Orchestra with Many Members**—Overview: The Wonderful Wet Machine, Ch. 2, pg. 53 The Cerebral Cortex: The Seat of the Mind, Ch. 2, pg. 59

	The Dual Brain: Thinking with Both Barrels, Ch. 2, pg. 62 Beneath the Cortex: The Inner Brain, Ch. 2, pg. 64 **Probing the Brain**—The Damaged Brain: What's Missing, Ch. 2, pg. 71

SENSATION

Hilton/Perdue **Allyn and Bacon Mind Matters CD**	**Kosslyn/Rosenberg** **Psychology: The Brain, The Person, The World**
Introduction to Sensation	**Sensing and Selecting: Opening Up to the World**—Sensation and Perception: Being in the World, Ch. 3, pg. 90
Sensory Transduction	**Sensing and Selecting: Opening Up to the World**—Psychophysics: A World of Experience, Ch. 3, pg. 92 **Vision**—Early Vision: It's Sensational!, Ch. 3, pg. 97 **Hearing**—Early Audition: If a Tree Falls but Nobody Hears It, Is There a Sound? Ch. 3, pg. 113 **Sensing in Other Ways**—Smell: A Nose for News? Ch. 3, pg. 120 Taste: The Mouth Has It, Ch. 3, pg. 121 Somasthetic Senses: Not Just Skin Deep, Ch. 3, pg. 122
Sensory Coding	**Vision**—Early Vision: It's Sensational! Ch. 3, Pg. 97 Intermediate Vision: Organizing the World, pg. 103 **Hearing**—Early Audition: If a Tree Falls but Nobody Hears It, Is There a Sound? Ch. 3, pg. 113 Intermediate Audition: Organizing the Auditory World, Ch. 3, pg. 116
Sensory Adaptation	**Vision**—Early Vision: It's Sensational! Ch. 3, pg. 97

PERCEPTION

Hilton/Perdue Allyn and Bacon Mind Matters CD	Kosslyn/Rosenbery
Introduction to Perception	**Sensing and Selecting: Opening Up to the World**—Sensation and Perception: Being in the World, Ch. 3, pg. 90 **Vision**—Intermediate Vision: Organizing the World, Ch. 3, pg. 103
Perceptual Constancy	**Vision**—Intermediate Vision: Organizing the World, Ch. 3, pg. 103 **Sensing and Selecting: Opening Up to the World**—Psychophysics: A World of Experience, Ch. 3, pg. 92
Perceptions as Decisions	**Vision**—Intermediate Vision: Organizing the World, Ch. 3, pg. 103
Perceptual Illusions	**Vision**—Intermediate Vision: Organizing the World, Ch. 3, pg. 103

LEARNING AND MEMORY

Hilton/Perdue Allyn and Bacon Mind Matters CD	Kosslyn/Rosenberg
Learning Through Association: Classical Conditioning	**Classical Conditioning**—Pavlov's Experiments, Ch. 5, pg. 167 Classical Conditioning: How It Works, Ch. 5, pg. 168 Classical Conditioning Applied, Ch. 5, pg. 172
Learning From Consequences: Operant Conditioning	**Operant Conditioning**, Ch. 5—Roots of Operant Conditioning: Its Discovery and How It Works, Ch. 5, pg. 177 Principles of Operant Conditioning, Ch. 5, pg. 178 Beyond Basic Reinforcement, Ch. 5, p. 182
Opening the Black Box: Cognitive Learning	**Classical Conditioning**—Classical Conditioning Applied, Ch. 5, pg. 172 **Cognitive and Social Learning**—Cognitive Learning, Ch. 5, pg. 190 Observational Learning: To See is to Know, Ch. 5, pg. 191 Learning from Models, Ch. 5, pg. 193 **Language: More Than Meets the Ear**—Language Development: Out of the Mouths of Babes, Ch. 7, pg. 241

	Mental Imagery: Perception Without Sensation, Ch. 7, pg. 249
Introduction to Memory	**Fact, Fiction and Forgetting: When Memory Goes Wrong**—Forgetting: Many Ways to Lose It, Ch. 6, pg. 223
The Memory Process	**Memory: A Many-Splendored Thing**—Storing Information, Ch. 6, pg. 200 **Encoding and Retrieving Information from Memory**—Making Memories, Ch. 6, pg.210 The Act of Remembering: Reconstructing Buried Cities, Ch. 6, pg. 215 **Fact, Fiction and Forgetting: When Memory Goes Wrong**—False Memories, Ch. 6, pg. 221 **Improving Memory: Tricks and Tools**—Storing Information Effectively: A Bag of Mnemonic Tricks, Ch. 6, pg. 227

BARON, *ESSENTIALS OF PSYCHOLOGY,* SECOND EDITION
HISTORY AND METHODS

Hilton/Perdue **Allyn and Bacon Mind Matters CD**	Baron **Essentials of Psychology 2E**
Psychology's Roots	Modern Psychology: What It Is and Where It Came From, Ch. 1, pg. 3
Recent Trends in Psychology	Psychologists: Who They Are and What They Do, Ch. 1, pg. 10
The Science of Psychology	Psychology and the Scientific Method, Ch. 1, pg. 13 The Scientific Method in Everyday Life: Thinking Critically About Human Behavior, Ch. 1, pg. 17 Research Methods in Psychology: How Psychologists Answer Questions About Behavior, Ch. 1, pg. 19 Extrasensory Perception: Perception without Sensation?, Ch. 4, pg. 117

BIOPSYCHOLOGY

Hilton/Perdue Allyn and Bacon Mind Matters CD	Baron Essentials of Psychology 2E
Evolution and Behavior	Heredity and Behavior, Ch. 2, pg. 69 Exploring Gender and Diversity, Ch. 10, pg. 356
Physiological Psychology: Neurons and the Endocrine System	Neurons: Building Blocks of the Nervous System, Ch. 2, pg. 41 The Endocrine System: Chemical Regulators of Bodily Processes, Ch. 2, pg. 66
Physiological Psychology: The Brain	The Brain: Where Consciousness is Manifest, Ch. 2, pg. 57 Lateralization of the Cerebral Cortex: Two Minds in One Body?, Ch. 2, pg. 63

SENSATION

Hilton/Perdue Allyn and Bacon Mind Matters CD	Baron Essentials of Psychology 2E
Introduction to Sensation	Sensation and Perception: Making Contact with the World around Us, Ch. 3, pg. 78
Sensory Transduction	Sensation: The Raw Materials of Understanding—Sensory Thresholds: How Much Stimulation is Enough?, Ch. 3, pg. 81 Vision—The Eye: Its Basic Structure, Ch. 3, pg. 84 Hearing—The Ear: Its Basic Structure, Ch. 3, pg. 91 Smell and Taste: The Chemical Senses, Ch. 3, pg. 99
Sensory Coding	Vision—Color Vision, Ch. 3, pg. 88 Vision—Vision and the Brain: Processing Visual Information, Ch. 3, pg. 90 Hearing–Pitch Perception, Ch. 3, pg. 93
Sensory Adaptation	Sensation: The Raw Materials of Understanding—Sensory Adaptation: "It Feels Great Once You Get Used to It," Ch. 3, pg. 83

PERCEPTION

Hilton/Perdue **Allyn and Bacon Mind Matters CD**	Baron **Essentials of Psychology 2E**
Introduction to Perception	Perception: Putting It All Together, Ch. 3, pg. 103
Perceptual Constancy	Perception: Putting It All Together — Constancies and Illusions: When Perception Succeeds–and Fails, Ch. 3, pg. 109
Perceptions as Decisions	Sensation: The Raw Materials of Understanding–Sensory Thresholds: How Much Stimulation is Enough?, Ch. 3, pg. 81 Perception: Putting It All Together —Some Key Perceptual Processes: Pattern and Distance, Ch. 3, pg. 113
Perceptual Illusions	Perception: Putting It All Together — Constancies and Illusions: When Perception Succeeds–and Fails, Ch. 3, pg. 115

LEARNING AND MEMORY

Hilton/Perdue **Allyn and Bacon Mind Matters CD**	Baron **Essentials of Psychology 2E**
Learning Through Association: Classical Conditioning	Classical Conditioning: Learning that Some Stimuli Signal Others, Ch. 5, pg. 164
Learning From Consequences: Operant Conditioning	Operant Conditioning: Learning Based on Consequences, Ch. 5, pg. 177 Research Methods: How Psychologists Study Applications of Operant Conditioning, Ch. 5, pg. 190
Opening the Black Box: Cognitive Learning	Observational Learning: Learning from the Behavior and Outcomes of Others, Ch. 5, pg. 194 Thinking: Forming Concepts and Reasoning to Conclusions, Ch. 7, pg. 256.
The Process of Remembering	Human Memory: The Information Processing Approach, Ch. 6, pg. 207 Sensory Memory, Short-Term Memory, and Long-Term Memory: Our Basic Memory Systems, Ch. 6, pg. 210 Memory Distortion and Memory Construction, Ch. 6, pg. 228

LEFTON, PSYCHOLOGY, Seventh Edition

HISTORY AND METHODS

Hilton/Perdue Allyn and Bacon Mind Matters CD	Lefton Psychology 7E
Psychology's Roots	How Have Schools of Psychological Thought Developed? Ch. 1, pg. 27
Recent Trends in Psychology	Psychological Schools Grow Broader, Ch. 1, pg. 29
The Science of Psychology	What Is This Science of Psychology? Ch. 1, pg. 3 The Research Process, Ch. 1, pg. 6

BIOPSYCHOLOGY

Hilton/Perdue Allyn and Bacon Mind Matters CD	Lefton Psychology 7E
Evolution and Behavior	Nature versus Nurture, Ch. 2, pg. 37 Psychological Schools Grow Broader—Evolutionary Psychology, Ch. 1, pg. 32
Physiological Psychology: Neurons and the Endocrine System	Communication in the Nervous System, Ch. 2, pg. 41 Hormones and Glands, Ch. 2, pg. 64
Physiological Psychology: The Brain	Brain Structures, Ch. 2, pg. 50

SENSATION

Hilton/Perdue Allyn and Bacon Mind Matters CD	Lefton Psychology 7E
Introduction to Sensation	The Perceptual Experience—Sensation and Perception: Definitions, Ch. 3, pg. 72
Sensory Transduction	The Perceptual Experience—Psychophysics, Ch. 3, pg. 73 The Visual System—The Structure of the Eye, Ch. 3, pg. 78 Hearing—Sound and Structure of the Ear, Ch. 3, pg. 96 Smell and Taste: The Chemical Senses, Ch. 3, pg. 103
Sensory Coding	Vision—Color Vision, Ch. 3, pg. 85 Hearing—Theories of Hearing, Ch. 3, pg. 99
Sensory Adaptation	Taste and Smell—Taste Ch. 3, pg. 101

Hilton/Perdue Allyn and Bacon Mind Matters CD	Lefton Psychology 7E
Introduction to Perception	Visual Perception—Gestalt Laws of Organization, Ch. 3, pg. 93
Perceptual Constancy	Visual Perception—Perception of Form: Constancy, Ch. 3, pg. 88
Perceptions as Decisions	The Perceptual Experience—Psychophysics, Ch. 3, pg. 73 Visual Perception—Depth Perception, Ch. 3, pg. 89
Perceptual Illusions	Visual Perception—Illusions, Ch. 3, pg. 92

LEARNING AND MEMORY

Hilton/Perdue Allyn and Bacon Mind Matters CD	Lefton Psychology 7E
Learning Through Association: Classical Conditioning	Pavlovian, or Classical, Conditioning Theory, Ch. 5, pg. 151 Key Variables in Classical Conditioning, Ch. 5, pg. 155
Learning From Consequences: Operant Conditioning	Operant Conditioning, Ch. 5, pg. 162 Key Variables in Operant Conditioning, Ch. 5, pg. 170
Opening the Black Box: Cognitive Learning	Cognitive Learning, Ch. 5, pg. 179
The Process of Remembering	Encoding, Ch. 6, pg. 192 Storage, Ch. 6, pg. 195 Retrieval, Ch. 6, pg. 204 Forgetting: When Memory Fails, Ch. 6, pg. 213

WOOD/WOOD, *THE WORLD OF PSYCHOLOGY,* THIRD EDITION

HISTORY AND METHODS

Hilton/Perdue Allyn and Bacon Mind Matters CD	Wood and Wood The World of Psychology 3E
Psychology's Roots	Exploring Psychology's Roots, Ch. 1, pg. 22
Recent Trends in Psychology	Psychology Today, Ch. 1, pg. 29
The Science of Psychology	Descriptive Research Methods, Ch. 1, pg. 7 The Experimental Method: Searching for Causes Ch. 1, pg. 10 Other Research Methods, Ch. 1, pg. 15 Subliminal Persuasion and Extrasensory Perception, Ch. 3, pg. 108

BIOPSYCHOLOGY

Hilton/Perdue Allyn and Bacon Mind Matters CD	Wood and Wood The World of Psychology 3E
Evolution and Behavior	The Expression of Emotion, Ch. 11, pg. 381
Physiological Psychology: Neurons and the Endocrine System	The Neurons and the Neurotransmitters, Ch. 2, pg. 38 The Endocrine System, Ch. 2, pg. 66
Physiological Psychology: The Brain	The Central Nervous System, Ch. 2, pg. 45 The Cerebral Hemispheres, Ch. 2, pg. 49 Brain Damage: Causes and Consequences, Ch. 2, pg. 62

SENSATION

Hilton/Perdue Allyn and Bacon Mind Matters CD	Wood and Wood The World of Psychology 3E
Introduction to Sensation	Sensation: The Sensory World, Ch. 3, pg. 74
Sensory Transduction	Sensation: The Sensory World — Transduction: Transforming Sensory Stimuli into Neural Impulses, Ch. 3, pg. 76 Sensation: The Sensory World —The Absolute Threshold: To Sense, or Not to Sense, Ch. 3, pg. 75. Sensation: The Sensory World —The Difference Threshold: Detecting Differences, Ch. 3, pg. 75
Sensory Coding	Vision—Color Vision: A Multicolored World, Ch. 3, pg. 82 Hearing—Sound: What We Here, Ch. 3, pg. 85
Sensory Adaptation	Sensation: The Sensory World—Sensory Adaptation, Ch. 3, pg. 76

PERCEPTION

Hilton/Perdue Allyn and Bacon Mind Matters CD	Wood and Wood The World of Psychology 3E
Introduction to Perception	Perception: Ways of Perceiving, Ch. 3, pg. 97
Perceptual Constancy	Perception: Ways of Perceiving—

	Perceptual Constancy, Ch. 3, pg. 99
Perceptions as Decisions	Sensation: The Sensory World–Signal Detection Theory, Ch. 3, pg. 76 Perception: Ways of Perceiving—Depth Perception: Perceiving What's Up Close and Far Away, Ch. 3, pg. 101 Perception: Ways of Perceiving—Perception of Motion, Ch. 3, pg. 103
Perceptual Illusions	Perception: Ways of Perceiving — Extraordinary Perceptions: Puzzling Perceptions, Ch. 3, pg. 104

LEARNING AND MEMORY

Hilton/Perdue Allyn and Bacon Mind Matters CD	Wood and Wood The World of Psychology 3E
Learning Through Association: Classical Conditioning	Classical Conditioning: The Original View, Ch. 5, pg. 152
Learning From Consequences: Operant Conditioning	Operant Conditioning, Ch. 5, pg. 165
Opening the Black Box: Cognitive Learning	Classical Conditioning: The Contemporary View, Ch. 5, pg. 160 Cognitive Learning, Ch. 5, pg. 181 Imagery and Concepts: Tools of Thinking, Ch. 7, pg. 228
The Process of Remembering	Remembering, Ch. 6, pg. 190. Measuring Memory, Ch. 6, pg. 198 The Nature of Remembering and Forgetting, Ch. 6, pg. 206 Factors Influencing Retrieval, Ch. 6, pg. 213

WOOD/WOOD, *THE ESSENTIAL WORLD OF PSYCHOLOGY*
HISTORY AND METHODS

Hilton/Perdue Allyn and Bacon Mind Matters CD	Wood and Wood The Essential World of Psychology
Psychology's Roots	Exploring Psychology's Roots, Ch. 1, pg. 17
Recent Trends in Psychology	Psychology Today, Ch. 1, pg. 22
The Science of Psychology	Descriptive Research Methods, Ch. 1, pg. 5 The Experimental Method: Searching for Causes Ch. 1, pg. 7 Other Research Methods, Ch. 1, pg. 12 Subliminal Persuasion and Extrasensory Perception, Ch. 3, pg. 88

BIOPSYCHOLOGY

Hilton/Perdue **Allyn and Bacon Mind Matters CD**	Wood and Wood **The Essential World of Psychology**
Evolution and Behavior	The Expression of Emotion, Ch. 9, pg. 310
Physiological Psychology: Neurons and the Endocrine System	The Neurons and the Neurotransmitters, Ch. 2, pg. 34 The Endocrine System, Ch. 2, pg. 54
Physiological Psychology: The Brain	The Central Nervous System, Ch. 2, pg. 39 The Cerebral Hemispheres, Ch. 2, pg. 43 Brain Damage: Causes and Consequences, Ch. 2, pg. 51

SENSATION

Hilton/Perdue **Allyn and Bacon Mind Matters CD**	Wood and Wood **The Essential World of Psychology**
Introduction to Sensation	Sensation: The Sensory World, Ch. 3, pg. 65
Sensory Transduction	Sensation: The Sensory World — Transduction: Transforming Sensory Stimuli into Neural Impulses, Ch. 3, pg. 67 Sensation: The Sensory World —The Absolute Threshold: To Sense, or Not to Sense, Ch. 3, pg. 66. Sensation: The Sensory World —The Difference Threshold: Detecting Differences, Ch. 3, pg. 66
Sensory Coding	Vision—Color Vision: A Multicolored World, Ch. 3, pg. 70 Hearing—Sound: What We Here, Ch. 3, pg. 73
Sensory Adaptation	Sensation: The Sensory World—Sensory Adaptation, Ch. 3, pg. 67

PERCEPTION

Hilton/Perdue **Allyn and Bacon Mind Matters CD**	Wood and Wood **The Essential World of Psychology**
Introduction to Perception	Perception: Ways of Perceiving, Ch. 3, pg. 80
Perceptual Constancy	Perception: Ways of Perceiving—Perceptual Constancy, Ch. 3, pg. 82
Perceptions as Decisions	Sensation: The Sensory World–Signal Detection Theory, Ch. 3, pg. 67 Perception: Ways of Perceiving—Depth

	Perception: Perceiving What's Up Close and Far Away, Ch. 3, pg. 83 Perception: Ways of Perceiving— Perception of Motion, Ch. 3, pg. 84
Perceptual Illusions	Perception: Ways of Perceiving — Extraordinary Perceptions: Puzzling Perceptions, Ch. 3, pg. 85

LEARNING AND MEMORY

Hilton/Perdue Allyn and Bacon Mind Matters CD	Wood and Wood The Essential World of Psychology
Learning Through Association: Classical Conditioning	Classical Conditioning: The Original View, Ch. 5, pg. 133
Learning From Consequences: Operant Conditioning	Operant Conditioning, Ch. 5, pg. 143
Opening the Black Box: Cognitive Learning	Classical Conditioning: The Contemporary View, Ch. 5, pg. 139 Cognitive Learning, Ch. 5, pg. 156 Imagery and Concepts: Tools of Thinking, Ch. 7, pg. 201
The Process of Remembering	Remembering, Ch. 6, pg. 168. Measuring Memory, Ch. 6, pg. 174 The Nature of Remembering and Forgetting, Ch. 6, pg. 178 Factors Influencing Retrieval, Ch. 6, pg. 184

ZIMBARDO/GERRIG, *PSYCHOLOGY AND LIFE,* FIFTEENTH EDITION

HISTORY AND METHODS

Hilton/Perdue Allyn and Bacon Mind Matters CD	Zimbardo/Gerrig 15E
Psychology's Roots	The Evolution of Modern Psychology— Psychology's Historical Foundations, Ch. 1
Recent Trends in Psychology	The Evolution of Modern Psychology— Current Psychological Perspectives, Ch. 1
The Science of Psychology	Psychological Research, Ch. 1

BIOPSYCHOLOGY

Hilton/Perdue Allyn and Bacon Mind Matters CD	Zimbardo/Gerrig 15E
Evolution and Behavior	Heredity and Behavior, Ch. 2
Physiological Psychology: Neurons and the Endocrine System	The Nervous System in Action Ch. 2 Biology and Behavior—The Endocrine

Physiological Psychology: The Brain	System, Ch. 2
	Biology and Behavior, Ch. 2 Hemispheric Specialization and Individual Differences, Ch. 2

SENSATION

Hilton/Perdue Allyn and Bacon Mind Matters CD	Zimbardo/Gerrig 15E

Introduction to Sensation	Identification and Recognition Processes—
	    Bottom-up and Top-down Processes, Ch.
	    4

Sensory Transduction	Sensory Knowledge of the World, Ch. 3
Sensory Coding	The Visual System—Seeing Color, Ch. 3 Hearing—Psychological Dimensions of Sound, Ch. 3
Sensory Adaptation	Sensory Knowledge of the World, Ch. 3

PERCEPTION

Hilton/Perdue Allyn and Bacon Mind Matters CD	Zimbardo/Gerrig 15E
Introduction to Perception	Organizational Processes in Perception— Principles of Perceptual Grouping, Ch. 4
Perceptual Constancy	Organizational Processes in Perception— Perceptual Constancies, Ch. 4

Perceptions as Decisions	Organizational Processes in Perception—
	    Depth Perception, Ch. 4
	Organizational Processes in Perception—
	    Motion Perception, Ch. 4

Perceptual Illusions	Sensing, Organizing, Indentifying, and
	    Recognizing—Reality, Ambiguity, and
	    Illusions, Ch. 4

LEARNING AND MEMORY

Hilton/Perdue Allyn and Bacon Mind Matters CD	Zimbardo/Gerrig 15E
Learning Through Association: Classical Conditioning	Classical Conditioning: Learning Predictable Signals, Ch. 6
Learning From Consequences: Operant Conditioning	Operant Conditioning: Learning About Consequences, Ch. 6
Opening the Black Box: Cognitive Learning	Cognitive Influences on Learning, Ch. 6
The Process of Remembering	What is Memory?, Ch. 7 Sensory Memory, Ch. 7 Short-Term Memory and Working Memory, Ch. 7

	Long-Term Memory: Encoding and Retrieval, Ch. 7
	Structures in Long-Term Memory—Remembering as a Reconstructive Process, Ch. 7

ZIMBARDO/WEBER/JOHNSON, *PSYCHOLOGY,* THIRD EDITION

HISTORY AND METHODS

Hilton/Perdue **Allyn and Bacon Mind Matters CD**	Zimbardo/Weber/Johnson **Psychology 3E**
Psychology's Roots and Recent Trends in Psychology	Where Does Modern Psychology Come From? Ch. 1, pg. 14-23
The Science of Psychology	How Do Psychologists Do Research?, Ch. 1, pg. 5-9, 24-34

BIOPSYCHOLOGY

Hilton/Perdue **Allyn and Bacon Mind Matters CD**	Zimbardo/Weber/Johnson **Psychology 3E**
Evolution and Behavior	How Are Genes and Behavior Linked?, Ch. 2, pg. 47-51 What Do Our Emotions Do for Us?, Ch. 8, pg. 47-52
Physiological Psychology: Neurons and the Endocrine System	How Does the Body Communicate Internally?—The Nervous System, Ch. 2, pg. 53-61 How Does the Body Communicate Internally?—The Endocrine System, Ch. 2, pg. 61-63
Physiological Psychology: The Brain	How Does the Brain Produce Behavior and Mental Processes, Ch. 2, pg. 64-72 How do the Cerebral Hemispheres Differ, Ch. 2, pg. 73-77

SENSATION

Hilton/Perdue **Allyn and Bacon Mind Matters CD**	Zimbardo/Weber/Johnson **Psychology 3E**
Introduction to Sensation	How Does Stimulation Become Sensation?, Ch. 5, pg. 163-168
Sensory Transduction	How Does Stimulation Become Sensation?—Transduction, Ch. 5, pg. 164-165 How Does Stimulation Become

	Sensation?—Thresholds, Ch. 5, pg. 166-167
Sensory Coding	How are the Senses Alike, and How are they Different?—Vision: How the Nervous System Processes Light Ch. 5, pg. 170-176
	How are the Senses Alike, and How are they Different?—Hearing: If a Tree Falls in a Forest…, Ch. 5, pg. 177-181
Sensory Adaptation	How Does Stimulation Become Sensation?—Sensory Adaptation, Ch. 5, pg. 165-166

PERCEPTION

Hilton/Perdue Allyn and Bacon Mind Matters CD	Zimbardo/Weber/Johnson Psychology 3E
Introduction to Perception	What is the Relationship Between Perception and Sensation?, Ch. 5, pg. 187-203
Perceptions as Decisions	How Does Stimulation Become Sensation?—Signal Detection Theory, Ch. 5, pg. 168-169
Perceptual Illusions	What is the Relationship Between Perception and Sensation?—Perceptual Ambiguity and Distortion, Ch. 5, pg. 190-193

LEARNING AND MEMORY

Hilton/Perdue Allyn and Bacon Mind Matters CD	Zimbardo/Weber/Johnson Psychology 3E
Learning Through Association: Classical Conditioning	How Does Classical Conditioning Explain Learning?, Ch. 6, pg. 212-219
Learning From Consequences: Operant Conditioning	How Do We Learn New Behaviors by Operant Conditioning, Ch. 6, pg. 220-229
Opening the Black Box: Cognitive Learning	How Does Cognitive Psychology Explain Learning?, Ch. 6, pg. 230-234
	How Do Cognitive Scientists Measure the Mind?, Ch. 7, pg. 231-234
The Process of Remembering	How Does Memory Work? Ch. 6, pg. 235-250

UNIT TABLES OF CONTENTS

HISTORY AND METHODS
Annotated Outline

I. Introduction
The history and methods unit begins by introducing psychology as a discipline concerned with explaining both ordinary and extraordinary behavior and mental activity.

A. The Big Questions
The introduction to psychology continues with three questions that frame the enormity of the task that confronts psychologists: What is the nature of the brain and its relationship to behavior? How can we use psychology to understand the very best and the very worst of human behavior? How do we come to know the world around us?

A1. ★The Mystery of the Human Mind
This is the first of three video clips that are intended to drive home the framing questions. In this clip, students see a brief narrated history of psychology beginning with pre-scientific approaches to understanding human behavior.

The Mystery of the Human Mind

Type of Activity: Movie

Learning Objective: Introduce students to the history of psychology.

Faculty Note: This is not intended as a detailed history, but more as a quick overview to stimulate thinking about the long history and diverse perspectives embodied in modern psychology.

Additional Resources:

Classics in the History of Psychology—This web site contains works of many classic psychologists including Watson, Pavlov, Freud, Titchner, Wundt, James, and many others. http://www.yorku.ca/dept/psych/classics/topic.htm

Major Events in the History of Psychology—This site contains an outline of the history of psychology. http://www.netaxs.com/people/aca3/lpm-hist.htm

The Letters of William James—Published by his son, these volumes contain many of the letters that William James wrote to friends, colleagues, and university officials. http://www.theatlantic.com/issues/96may/nitrous/jamii.htm

Timetable of significant events in Psychology—As advertised, this site contains a good outline of the history of psychology. http://paradigm.soci.brocku.ca/~lward/TIME/TIME_PSY.HTML

Today in the History of Psychology—This site allows you to enter a date and see what happened in psychology on that date. http://www.cwu.edu/~warren/calendar/datepick.html

---

A2. ★Studying Human Nature

This video clip contains footage from the Los Angeles Riots. Examples of aggression and self-sacrifice are included in the clips.

Studying Human Nature
Type of Activity: Movie
Learning Objective: Encourage students to think about how we might begin to explain the diversity of human behavior.
Faculty Note: Extreme circumstances reveal interesting facets of human behavior. In this video clip, students can see footage from the L.A. riots. These riots revealed the power of social situations to foster antisocial behavior, and yet at the same time they contained numerous instances of individual altruism and prosocial behavior. It may be useful to point out here that while observation of abnormal behavior or the behavior of individuals in abnormal situations may prove valuable, many psychologists are also interested in "normal" behavior and the more typical situations in which people find themselves.
The same point can be made about other areas, such as studies of perception. Research on both normal perceptual processes and unusual perceptual processes (e.g., illusions, hallucinations, etc.) contribute to our overall understanding.

A3. ★What Is This?

This video contains a visual illusion. It is included to help students see that much of our everyday life is not nearly as obvious as it first appears.

What is This?
Type of Activity: Movie
Learning Objective: Encourage students to think about the role that context and situations play in shaping psychological experiences.
Faculty Note: The goal of this clip is to help students see that perception, and, more generally, psychological experience are relative. The video shows what appears to be a light "hopping" across the screen. But when another light is added as a reference point, it creates a very different perception as the light now appears to rotate across the screen.
This same video clip could be shown during discussions of the Gestalt perspective as it demonstrates the organizing principles we impose on perception.

II. Psychology's Roots

A. Structuralism: The Mind Is a Molecule

In this section, Structuralism, with its emphasis on finding the basic elements of conscious experience and reliance upon introspection is highlighted.

B. Functionalism: The Mind Is a Tool

Functionalism is introduced as a uniquely American school of psychology. Unlike structuralists, functionalists like William James argued that it is not possible to study the mind and behavior without understanding the functions that they serve.

C. Psychoanalysis: The Mind Is an Iceberg

Described as one of the great upheavals in human thought, the psychoanalytic perspective challenged the notion that behavior is primarily under the control of conscious thought. Instead, Freud argued that the unconscious is the driving force behind many of our behaviors.

D. Behaviorism: Psychology Loses Its Mind

In 1913, John Watson mounted an assault on what he perceived as the unscientific mysticism and mentalism of psychology. He and his fellow behaviorists argued that psychology should be concerned with the study of observable behaviors and the environments in which they occur.

E. Gestalt Psychology: The Mind Is More Than Meets the Eye

Unlike the behaviorist, Gestalt psychologists continued to argue for the need to study consciousness. In studies of illusions and perceptual constancies, they believed that they saw evidence of a mind that actively organizes and structures perception. In their terms, the perception is greater than the sum or its sensory parts.

F. Humanism: The Mind Has Potential

Sometimes called the Third Force in psychology, humanistic psychology emerged in response to the pessimistic views of human nature embodied in psychoanalysis and behaviorism. Humanistic psychologists emphasized the freedom of individuals to make choices and change their lives for the better.

G. Schools of Psychology: Recess

In this section, students can learn more about many of the leading figures in psychology and review their knowledge of the schools of psychology.

G1. ★Pop-Up: Schools of Psychology Matching Game

Although sharing the goal of establishing a viable science of psychology, the first psychologists were often divided by arguments about the proper methods and subject matter of the field. In this game, students try to match some of the early theorists to the theories they advocated.

Schools of Psychology Matching Game
Type of Activity: Interactive Animation
Learning Objective: Reinforce students' mastery of the schools of psychology.
Faculty Note: In this activity, students can test their knowledge of the different schools of thought by matching the schools with their perspectives.

G2. ★Pop-Up: All-Star Psychologists

In this pop-up, students can take a somewhat whimsical tour of the contributions of many leading figures in the field.

III. Recent Trends in Psychology

A. Cognitive Psychology

By the mid-1950's, many psychologists had come to the conclusion that the behaviorists' approach was inadequate. Using the computer as a metaphor, cognitive psychologists began studying the ways that the mind interprets, processes, and stores information. Cognitive psychology embraces "mentalism" and it is currently one of the most influential paradigms in psychology.

B. Biopsychology

The other major trend in recent years has been an expanded interest in the evolutionary, physiological, and biochemical influences on behavior. This interest has been stimulated by our increasing knowledge of neurotransmitters, the development of more sophisticated procedures for measuring the structures and functions of the brain, and the emergence of evolutionary-based theories that are open to testing and refutation.

B1. ★Depression Among the Amish

In this video clip, students can see a summary account of one attempt to trace the inheritance of mood disorders.

Depression Among the Amish

Activity Type: Movie

Learning Objective: Introduce the notion that biology influences human behavior.

Faculty Note: In this video, students learn about one attempt to find a genetic cause for a mood disorder. Although many psychologists are convinced that a predisposition towards these disorders may be inherited, more recent attempts to identify the precise location of a specific "depression gene" have been unsuccessful. This subsequent failure to find a specific gene provides an opportunity to talk about the promise and limitations of the biopsychological approach to understanding behavior.

The instructor may want to return to this in other sections of the course as well, such as in a discussion of the medical model of psychological disorders. One question to ask students might be: If a disorder can be inherited, exactly **what** is passed on—a neurotransmitter imbalance? a structural flaw in the brain? hormonal differences?

It might be pointed out that some disorders have a more obvious genetic component (e.g., schizophrenia, certain forms of dementia, bipolar disorder, etc.) while others appear to be much less influenced by genetic predispositions.

Another potentially relevant topic would be the possible genetic contributions to personality traits. If predispositions toward emotional problems can be inherited, why not predispositions towards introversion, extraversion, or friendliness?

Additional Resources:

NAMI—this site, maintained by the National Alliance for the Mentally Ill, contains an update on the search for genetic links to bipolar disorder. http://laami.nami.org/disorder/disordg.htm

C. Psychology's Careers and Branches

Modern psychology is a broad field. A 1993 survey of the nearly 120,000 members of the American Psychological Association found them working in 236 different specialty areas.

C1. ★Branches of Psychology

In this activity, students can explore a variety of specialties in psychology.

Careers in Psychology

Type of Activity: Interactive Illustration

Learning Objective: Allow students to explore the specialties and sub-disciplines of psychology.

Faculty Note: This "family tree" of psychological specialties should help convince students that the field of psychology accommodates a great variety of interests, and that almost all facets of human behavior are fair game for inquiries by psychologists.

Of course, even this relatively large "tree" does not cover all specialties, or the forms that they may take in other disciplines such as economics, decision sciences, political science, criminology, business, etc.

Additional Resources:

The American Psychological Association web site can be found at http://www.apa.org

The American Psychological Society web site can be found at http://www.psychologicalscience.org

---

C2. ★What Is Psychology?

As diverse as psychology is, two threads link its various branches. The first is the idea that psychologists are concerned with the scientific study of human behavior. The second is the understanding that the various branches of psychology share a common history. The video presented here illustrates some of the diverse elements of psychology.

What is Psychology?

Activity Type: Movie

Learning Objective: Portray the diversity of subject matter and research methods among modern psychologists.

Faculty Note: This video provides a quick montage of segments showing different types of psychological inquiries, such as those conducted in clinical and laboratory settings. It is not intended to be a comprehensive review of methodology. However, it may be instructive to have students guess what questions the psychologists in the segments are investigating.

Rapid Review 1

IV. THE SCIENCE OF PSYCHOLOGY

The remainder of this unit is designed to introduce students to the principles and methods of scientific psychology.

A. Common Sense vs. Scientific Psychology

Psychology is often accused of being nothing more than common sense. In this section, the shortcomings of common sense are highlighted and psychology is distinguished from common sense on the basis of psychology's commitment to the principles of science.

A1. ★Pop-Up: Predicting the Results of Psychological Research

This section introduces an activity that allows students to test the accuracy of their common sense predictions. For most students, their common sense predictions will be poor predictors of their actual behavior.

Predicting the Results of Psychological Research

Type of Activity: Simulation

Learning Objective: Encourage students to think critically about the differences between "common sense" views of behavior and psychological accounts of behavior.

Faculty Note: In the activity, students see the solutions to several anagrams (i.e., scrambled words) and are asked to predict how long it would have taken them to solve the anagrams had they not seen the solutions. Because of hindsight bias (i.e., the answers seem obvious once known) most students will underestimate the amount of time it takes to solve these anagrams. They are then given a chance to actually complete several anagrams and their actual times are measured. The point that the activity makes is that we are often in the position of having known what happens when we try to understand psychological phenomena. The challenge to scientific psychology is to predict processes in advance.

Sometimes, after being told of the conclusions reached by researchers, students respond that they had known them all along, or as if the outcomes were predictable. This exercise might be part of an antidote to this sort of hindsight bias. In line with this, it may be useful to remind your students of this when discussing early classical conditioning research, such as Pavlov's conditioning of salivation in dogs or the Little Albert experiment conducted by John Watson. The results of these studies may appear obvious or predictable to modern observers, but represented radically unconventional ideas at the time they were first presented. On the flip side, a number of studies continue to be surprising including Milgram's work on obedience, Nisbett and Wilson's work on explaining our own behavior, and much of the cognitive dissonance literature.

B. The Scientific Method

In this section the scientific method is described as a process that involves observation, theory construction, hypothesis generation, and data collection. Darley and Latané's work on bystander intervention is then presented as a case study in how the scientific method unfolds.

C. Having an Attitude

Using the scientific method also involves adopting a certain set of attitudes. Scientists are skeptical, always on the lookout for alternative explanations for what they observe. Similarly, scientists seek parsimony. As Einstein put it, "Everything should be made as simple as possible, but not any simpler."

C1. ★Pop-Up: Evidence and Psychic Abilities

Using themselves as subjects, students can apply the scientific method to claims of paranormal activities.

Evidence of Psychic Abilities

Type of Activity: Simulation

Learning Objective: Learn to apply the scientific method to psychological questions.

Faculty Note: Students are given an opportunity to take part in a "test" of their precognitive or clairvoyant abilities using the stimuli from Zener cards (circle, square, star, cross, and wavy lines). After the student makes a series of attempts to predict which of the cards the computer will present, their frequency of "hits" can be compared to the number expected by chance alone. It should be noted that whenever a hypothesis is tested scientifically, we should have a clear idea what would constitute sufficient evidence to reject the null hypothesis.

It should also be made clear to the students that "evidence" for or against extraordinary claims (such as claims of psychic abilities) must be objective and quantifiable, and should be decided upon beforehand. Anecdotes are not enough.

If by chance a student scores enough "hits" to make it appear as if something extraordinary is happening, instructors might want to remind him or her that a critical task in science is the **replication** of interesting results to insure against accidents, and then suggest repeat attempts.

Additional Resources:

Perhaps the only published article in an APA journal to make claims in support of ESP is Daryl Bem's work in *Psychological Bulletin*. Bem, D. J., and Honorton, C. (1994). Does psi exist? Replicable evidence for an anomalous process of information transfer. Psychological Bulletin, 115, 4-18

Bem also has a web page that can be found at http://www.psych.cornell.edu/dbem/online_pubs.html. This page even has a non-specialist's guide to the article.

Rapid Review 2

D. Collecting Evidence in Psychology

The actual techniques employed by psychologists to collect evidence vary widely depending on the area of psychology and the question being asked. This section reviews basic concepts involved in data collection including: descriptive and experimental data; field and laboratory studies; case studies; surveys; naturalistic observations; correlations and experiments; and random assignment and random sampling. Where appropriate, pop-ups are used to reinforce the concepts.

D1. ★A Case Study in Schizophrenia

This video clip contains a case study interview with a woman suffering from schizophrenia.

A Case Study in Schizophrenia

Type of Activity: Movie

Learning Objective: See an example of the case study method in psychology.

Faculty Note: While this is only a highly abbreviated case study, it does emphasize the personal, individual nature of this approach, as well as the humanizing effect of focusing on the individual instead of the disorder.

Pioneering personality theorist Gordon Allport made the point that while nomothetic research (the search for general laws and principles in large populations) is crucial in science, psychologists should never lose sight of the uniqueness and importance of the individual; they should also conduct idiographic inquiries (case studies).

Additional Resources:

Schizophrenia Resources-NAMI—This site, maintained by the National Alliance for the Mentally Ill, contains a list of schizophrenia resources and links.
http://schizophrenia.nami.org/schizophrenia/schizophrenia.html

D2. ★Pop—Up: Interactive Correlation

In this activity, students can explore the correlational concepts of size, direction, and causality.

Interactive Correlation
Type of Activity: Exploration
Learning Objective: Help students master concepts related to correlation.
Faculty Note: . Some of the most interesting ideas in the field started out as statements about a relationship between two variables: Conformity correlates with group size, dreaming correlates with REM sleep, recall correlates with depth of processing, job performance correlates with achievement motivation, IQ test scores correlate with school performance, etc. The concept of a correlation between variables is critical to many areas of psychology.
The most important limitation to emphasize is probably the fact that correlation does not always imply causation. Although ice cream sales are correlated with the number of drowning deaths on any given day, we can't necessarily assume that the ice cream is causing the drownings. A third variable, daily temperature, would seem to explain the connection between the two.
Additional Resources:
Guessing Correlations—This site allows students to play a game in which they guess correlations. http://www.stat.uiuc.edu/~stat100/java/guess/GCApplet.html

D3. ★The Milgram Obedience Experiment

This video contains archival footage of Stanley Milgram's famous "Obedience to Authority Experiment." In the study, Milgram attempted to determine if the close proximity of an authority figure (the independent variable) could cause even normal individuals to engage in acts of destructive obedience (the dependent variable). Prior to this study, almost no one anticipated the degree to which these subjects would commit harmful acts at the request of such an authority.

The Milgram Obedience Experiment
Type of Activity: Movie
Learning Objective: Help students see the power that experiments have to establish the causes of behavior, and to uncover surprising and counter-intuitive findings.
Faculty Note: In this study Milgram found that even average, mentally healthy persons will (apparently) inflict great pain on another subject at the command of an experimenter. The Milgram experiment can be used to stimulate discussion on a variety of topics:
Finding a way to study destructive obedience in the laboratory was an innovative approach to understanding this phenomenon. Some critics were initially concerned about the external validity of the study: However, subsequent research has shown that the results do generalize to other real-world settings.
Prior to the study, Milgram described his experiment to a variety of psychologists and laypersons and asked them to predict what the subjects would do. Almost nobody believed that "normal" individuals would follow harmful orders to that degree. In fact, more than 60 percent obeyed to the end.

D4. ★The Lewin Leadership Study

This video contains archival footage of Kurt Lewin's groundbreaking use of experimental methods to discover the consequences of different leadership styles. In this study, children were randomly assigned to different groups, each governed by a different type of leader. Since membership in the groups was randomly determined, any differences between the groups that emerged during the study could be attributed to the effects of the leaders.

The Lewin Leadership Study
Type of Activity: Movie
Learning Objective: Help students see that behavior as complicated as "democracy" can be studied scientifically.
Faculty Note: In this study, children were randomly assigned to different groups, each governed by a different type of leader. Since membership in the groups was randomly determined, any differences between the groups that emerged during the study could be attributed to the effects of the leaders.
One element of this study that is worth noting is the subject matter. Lewin was insistent that the results of psychological research should help us with practical, real-world problems such as those of leadership and government.
Another point worth noting is the importance of random assignment to the experiment. The different leadership styles could not be fairly compared if the subjects were allowed to volunteer for particular groups. Random assignment allows you to assume that the groups in the study start out the same.

D5. ★Pop-Up: A Methodological Decision Tree

Psychologists use a variety of research methods. Each method has its advantages and disadvantages. In this activity, students are encouraged to consider the proposition that violent TV programming leads to increased levels of aggression among children. They are then encourage to use a decision tree to explore a variety of methods that could be used to test the proposition.

A Methodological Decision Tree
Type of Activity: Exploration
Learning Objective: Allow students to make decisions about what methodologies can be applied to a common research question and illustrate how the conclusions one can draw from a study depend upon the methods used.
Faculty Note: It is often useful to pick a famous study in psychology (such as the Milgram obedience study, the Little Albert study, Shepard's mental rotation study, Ebbinghaus' study on memory retention, or the Phineas Gage case study), to see how the basic questions addressed in that study might have been explored using other methods.

Rapid Review 3

BIOPSYCHOLOGY TABLE OF CONTENTS

BIOPSYCHOLOGY
Annotated Outline

I. Introduction to Biopsychology
The Biopsychology unit begins with a distinction between proximal and distal causes. Proximal causes of a behavior are its immediate causes. When applied to biological explanations, proximal causes focus on the ways in which physiological changes shape the organism's behavior and psychological experience. Distal causes of behavior are its remote causes. When applied to biological explanations, distal causes focus on the ways in which the evolutionary heritage of the organism shapes behavior and psychological experience.

I1. ★Pop-Up: Bio-Fallacies
Through a combination of text and graphics, students are introduced to the nominal fallacy, the deterministic fallacy, naturalistic fallacy, and the false war between nature and nurture fallacy.

Bio-Fallacies

Activity Type: Illustrated Essay
Learning Objective: Encourage critical thinking about biological explanations of behavior.
Faculty Note: The **nominal fallacy** occurs when a phenomenon is simply renamed or labeled rather than understood. The **deterministic fallacy** occurs when someone concludes that genetics rigidly prescribe behavior. The **naturalistic fallacy** occurs when someone concludes that something is good because it occurs naturally. The **false war between nature and nurture** is a fallacy that involves pitting nature and nurture explanations against each other. Behavior is almost always influenced by an interaction between nature and nurture.

II. Evolution and Behavior
The notion that some behaviors may be explained by evolution is introduced by pointing out that people are much more likely to develop a fear of snakes, which annually kill approximately 15 U.S. citizens, than one of automobiles, which annually kill approximately 43,000 U.S. citizens.

A. Darwin's Theory of Evolution and Principle of Natural Selection
This section briefly introduces students to Darwin's notions of adaptation and natural selection.

A1. ★Pop-up: A Profile of Charles Darwin
This pop-up contains a brief biography of Darwin.

> ### A Profile of Charles Darwin
> **Type of Activity:** Illustrated Essay
> **Learning Objective:** Introduce students to Darwin and provide context for his theory of evolution by natural selection.
> **Faculty Note:** Darwin is, of course, remembered for his theory of evolution by natural selection. Most students probably know this from other classes. What students often don't know is what Darwin was like as a person. One of the goals of this pop-up is to humanize Darwin. He led a fascinating life. For example, his mother was the daughter of the founder of the Wedgwood china works. Similarly, Darwin was an unspectacular student while in college. And, although he spent five years traveling about the H.M.S. Beagle serving as the ship's naturalist after completing college, for the rest of his life he rarely traveled.
> **Additional Resources:** Darwin's *Voyage of the Beagle* and *The Origin of Species* can be found at http://www.literature.org/Works/Charles-Darwing/

B. Assumptions of Natural Selection

What separated Darwin's theory of evolution from other theories of adaptation was the principle of natural selection. This section presents four assumptions that are contained in natural selection. 1) Individual members of a species vary from one another. 2) Some characteristics are passed on genetically. 3) Some characteristics aid survival and reproduction. 4) For selection to take place, a characteristic must affect the rate of reproductive success.

B1. ★Pop-up: Cyberlemmings: A simulation of the Natural Selection Process

In this pop-up, students can explore the effects that varying selection pressure and time have on the rate of acrophobia in a mythical population of cyberlemmings.

> ### Cyberlemmings: A simulation of the Natural Selection Process
> **Type of Activity:** Simulation
> **Learning Objective:** Understand the concept of natural selection and how it influences evolution across generations.
> **Faculty Note:** The goal of this activity to help students understand how natural selection could shape a particular behavior: in this case, fear of heights. When students first observe the cyberlemmings, they see a gaggle of them milling about randomly near the edge of a cliff, with some periodically straying too close and falling over. Some of the cyberlemmings are somewhat acrophobic. They are labeled with a yellow streak down their backs and they tend to stay farther from the edge. After observing the cyberlemmings, the students can then change the selection pressure by raising or lowering the height of the cliff and observe the effects that these changes have on subsequent generations of cyberlemmings. If selection pressure is low (i.e., if the cliff is low and therefore not lethal) the proportion of acrophobic lemmings will not change across generations. In contrast, if the selection pressure is high (i.e., if the cliff is tall and lethal) the proportion of acrophobic lemmings will tend to increase across generations. How quickly that increase occurs depends upon the magnitude of the selection pressure. The greater the selection pressure, the faster the change.
> One of the main points of this simulation is to help students to see that evolution happens slowly, across thousands of generations. Students sometimes ask, for example, if recent inventions like the automobile have caused humans to evolve in ways that are different from our ancestors. From an evolutionary perspective, the clear answer is "not yet." The introduction of the automobile is far too recent to have affected the course of human evolution in any measurable way.
> The computer simulation gets around the problem of the slow pace of evolution by looking at slices in time separated by thousands of generations. In real life, we can get around that problem by looking at organisms that have quick generations. For example, although we cannot observe

evolution happening in real time with humans, a feature that makes it difficult to test evolutionary accounts of human behavior, we can see it happening among bacteria. The growing number of antibiotic resistant strains of bacteria provides strong support for Darwin's principle of natural selection.

Additional Resources:
Richard Dawkins, *The Blind Watchmaker*, provides an interesting tour of evolutionary principles. If you are interested in other simulations of natural selection processes try the biology simulation page at http://biology.miningco.com/msub16.htm

C. Natural Selection and Behavior

This section continues with the idea that evolution not only shapes anatomy, it may also shape behavior.

C1. ★Pop-up: The Universality of Emotions

In this pop-up, students can try their hands at Ekman's emotion naming task. Ekman and Friesen (1975) found strong agreement across many cultures in the identification of fear, joy, anger, disgust, sadness, and surprise, suggesting that these "primary" emotions may have their basis in evolution.

The Universality of Emotions

Type of Activity: Exploration

Learning Objective: Introduce students to the notion that some emotions are universal and possibly the product of evolution.

Faculty Note: In this activity, the students' task it to match photos of people expressing a variety of emotions with the appropriate emotion label. The photos and labels that are used involve six "universal" emotions identified by Ekman (i.e., anger, fear, happiness, disgust, sadness, and surprise). Because these emotions are universal, students should have little difficulty matching them correctly. At the end of the activity, they can look at results from cross-cultural studies of emotions.

A point that often comes up in the discussion of emotions is whether all emotions are similar across all cultures. Although there is good evidence that these six emotions hold true across vastly different cultures, the cross-cultural evidence for other "secondary" emotions (e.g., love or pride) is less compelling. Indeed, though not statistically significant, the cross-cultural data presented in this activity suggest that even among the primary emotions, cross-cultural agreement is lower for the negative emotions than for the positive emotions. This trend provides an opportunity to discuss the roles that culture plays in shaping both the experience and expression of emotions.

Additional Resources:
Emotion Laboratory Research—This site discusses ways to study emotions.
http://www.psy.ulaval.ca/~arvid/R2e.html

D. The Evolution of Dating and Altruism

In this section, an evolutionary account of altruism is proposed. From the standpoint of evolution, altruism is only adaptive if it facilitates the transmission of the altruist's genes to the next generation. The principle of "kin selection" (i.e., the notion that we tend to help similar others) may provide one such mechanism of transmission.

D. ★Pop-up: Studying Mate Selection

In this pop-up, the characteristics that males and females look for in potential partners are explored from an evolutionary perspective. According to evolutionary theorists, differences emerge because of the different selection pressures that confront men and women. For men, the easiest way to maximize reproductive success would be to mate with as many fertile women as possible. In contrast, the route to reproductive success for women would be to ensure the survival of the relatively few offspring they can bear. The activity that is included in the pop-up asks students to guess the gender of the authors of a collection of personal ads that vary in their emphasis on status versus physical attractiveness.

Studying Mate Selection

Type of Activity: Exploration

Learning Objective: Introduce students to an evolutionary account of a complex human behavior. The goal is to help students to see the logic behind evolutionary-based explanations and to help them to think critically about the relationship between evolution and behavior.

Faculty Note: Evolutionary accounts of human behavior are often controversial. This is particularly true when the behavior in question is something as complex and mysterious as love. In this activity, students try to guess the gender of the authors of a series of personal ads. On average, the ads written by males indicate an interest in finding a younger and physically attractive partner, while the ads written by females indicate an interest in finding an older, financially secure partner. Evolutionary psychologists argue that this difference has its origins in the different selection pressures that have confronted men and women. Because fertility varies as a function of age more among women than among men, for men the pressure has been to find fertile mates. According to this argument, because there is no clear indicator of fertility of humans, youth and beauty have become the proxies that signal fertility. In contrast, because the physical demands of birth fall disproportionately on women, evolutionary psychologists have argued that the pressure on women has been to find mates who can contribute to the protection of any offspring. In psychological terms, this translates to a preference for high-status, emotionally committed men.

In teaching evolutionary accounts of behavior, particularly when those accounts focus on gender differences, it is often worth reminding students of several things. First, although men and women do sometimes behave differently, we are far more similar than we are different. For example, although men may focus relatively more on physical features while women focus more on status and commitment, most men and women would prefer someone who is physically attractive and high in status. Second, students should keep the deterministic fallacy in mind. Even if evolution has shaped preferences, this does not mean that an individual is hostage to his or her evolutionary heritage. Third, students should also keep the naturalistic fallacy in mind. There is a tendency to assume that if something is the product of evolution, it is a good thing. Evolution and worth have nothing to do with each other.

Additional Resources:

One question that the mate selection research raises is "What is beauty?" A 1996 article by D. Singh pitted Waist to Hip Ratio (WHR) against overall weight to see how much each varies by time. Using archival data, Singh found that WHR, which is correlated with fertility, has stayed fairly constant across time and culture. In contrast weight, which is not correlated with fertility, varies considerably across time and culture. His web site can be found http://www.psy.utexas.edu/psy/FACULTY/Singh/Singh.html

---

E. Natural Selection and Snake Phobia

The evolution section ends where it began, with a consideration of the evolutionary account of snake phobia. In 1971, Seligman proposed that individuals who tended to avoid snakes might have had a greater chance of surviving and passing that tendency on to their offspring. Over many generations, the proportion of "phobic" individuals would have increased.

Rapid Review 1

III. Physiological Psychology

This section introduces the search for proximal causes of behavior, beginning with the nervous system.

A. Neurons: The Building Blocks of the Nervous System

In this section, neurons are introduced as cells that specialize in communication.

B. The Structure of a Neuron

This section divides neurons into three parts: the soma, which functions to keep the cell alive; the dendrites, which receive messages from nearby neurons; and the axon, which transmits information down the length of the neuron.

B1. ★The Rollover Neuron

In this interactive animation, students can explore the functions of various parts of the neuron.

The Rollover Neuron
Type of Activity: Interactive Illustration
Learning Objective: Learn and remember the major anatomical structures in a neuron including the dendrites, cell body, axon, and synapse.
Faculty Note: In this activity, students can explore the anatomy of a neuron by rolling their cursors over various structures in the neuron and seeing the names of the various structures pop up.

C. Types of Neurons

In this section, sensory neurons, motor neurons, and interneurons are all identified.

D. How Neurons Operate

All neurons are described as transmitting information in the same manner, by a combination of electrical and chemical processes. In this section, the resting state of the neuron is described.

E. The Action Potential

This section describes the changes that a neuron goes through as an action potential is generated.

F. Crossing the Synapse

This section describes the changes that occur when an action potential reaches the synapse between two neurons.

G. At the Receiving Neuron

This section describes the changes that occur at the receiving neuron (a.k.a., the post-synaptic neuron) as neurotransmitters bind at receptor cites.

G1. ★Pop-up: The Navigable Neuron

In this activity, students can explore the operation of neurons through a series of interactive animations and text.

The Navigable Neuron
Type of Activity: Exploration
Learning Objective: Discover the functions that various anatomical structures in a neuron perform.
Faculty Note: This activity is designed to reinforce and extend the rollover neuron animation that precedes it. In the rollover neuron animation, students are drilled on the names of the various parts of a neuron. In this activity, students can click on the various structures within a neuron and see animated descriptions of what a particular structures does.
Additional Resources: Neurosciences on the Internet—This site contains links to a variety or resources and also has a searchable database. http://www.neuroguide.com/

G2. ★Pop-up: An Exercise in Neural Communication

In this activity, students can explore the concept of the "graded potential" in greater detail by seeing what happens with various combinations of excitatory and inhibitory messages.

An Exercise in Neural Communication
Type of Activity: Exploration
Learning Objective: Understand excitation, inhibition, and the graded potential.
Faculty Note: While the navigable neuron helps students to explore an individual neuron, it does not capture the interaction between neurons. This activity is designed to help students see how neurons influence each other by allowing them to examine the conditions that lead an animated post-synaptic neuron to fire. In the activity, students will see a schematic of a neuron that includes the soma, dendrites, and axon hillock of a neuron. In addition, they will see an electrical gauge that measures the activity inside the neuron. The students' task in the activity is to experiment with different combinations of fast and slow excitatory and inhibitory inputs and observe the effect these inputs have on the post-synaptic neuron. Completing the activity should help students gain a better understanding of the graded potential and of the action potential threshold.
Additional Resources: A series of online neural tutorials can be found at http://psych.hanover.edu/Krantz/neurotut.html

H. Neurotransmitters

This section describes neurotransmitters and their functions.

H1. ★Neurotransmitter Effects

In this activity, students can explore the behavioral effects of various neurotransmitters.

Neurotransmitter Effects
Type of Activity: Interactive Illustration
Learning Objective: Learn and remember the physiological and psychological effects of selected neurotransmitters.
Faculty Note: In this activity, students can explore the behavioral effects of various neurotransmitters by clicking on the neurotransmitter and seeing a description of its behavioral and psychological effects.
Additional Resources: A gallery of animations depicting the actions of neurotransmitters at the synapse is available at http://www.neuroguide.com/cajal_gallery.html

H2. ★Pop-up: How Cocaine Works

In this video, students can see an animation of the effects that cocaine has at the synapse. In large part, the feeling of intense pleasure that cocaine produces is due to cocaine's ability to block re-uptake of dopamine.

How Cocaine Works
Type of Activity: Movie
Learning Objective: Understand how neurotransmitters operate at the synapse and the effects that cocaine has on this process.
Faculty Note: This video clip contains an excellent animation of neurotransmitters crossing the synaptic cleft and binding on the post-synaptic neuron. The explanation about re-uptake and the effects that cocaine has on that process is engaging and frequently provokes questions. The video provides a good context for determining how well students understand the behavior of neurons and neurotransmitters.
Additional Resources: Another animation of cocaine blocking dopamine re-uptake can be found at http://www.neuroguide.com/newpump.html

I. The Endocrine System

In this section, the structure and function of the endocrine system is described.

I1. ★Elements of the Endocrine System

In this activity, students can explore the structure and functions of various parts of the endocrine system.

> **Elements of the Endocrine System**
>
> **Type of Activity:** Interactive Animation
>
> **Learning Objective:** Learn and remember the functions of the major anatomical structures in the endocrine system.
>
> **Faculty Note:** In this activity, students can explore the structure of the endocrine system by rolling their cursors over various parts of the endocrine system and seeing their names and functions appear on screen.

Rapid Review 2

IV. Physiological Psychology: The Brain

In this section, the brain is discussed as a complex structure that is composed of a variety of specialized parts. The subsequent discussion of the functions of those parts is organized around the division between the central and peripheral nervous systems and the emergence of the hindbrain, midbrain, and forebrain.

A. The Structure of the Nervous System

In this section, the structure of the nervous system is described.

A1. ★Pop-up: The Classic Case of Phineas Gage

One of the first cases to provide insight into the relationships between the various structures of the brain and behavior was the case of Phineas Gage. The story of his injury and behavioral changes that followed are chronicled in this pop-up.

> **The Classic Case of Phineas Gage**
>
> **Type of Activity:** Illustrated Essay
>
> **Learning Objective:** Introduce students to the notion that specific parts of the brain are involved in specific behaviors and psychological experiences.
>
> **Faculty Note:** Phineas Gage was a construction foreman for the Rutland and Burlington Railroad in Vermont when he had an accident that resulted in an iron bar being blown through the front of his head. Although he survived the accident, his subsequent behavior and personality were quite different. His case is historically important because it provides one of the first attempts to link brain damage to specific changes in behavior and personality.
>
> **Additional Resources:** An entire web site devoted to Phineas Gage can be found at http://www.psych.unimelb.edu.au/phineas_gage.html

B. The Hindbrain

In this section, the functions of the various structures of that make up the hindbrain (i.e., the medulla, pons, and cerebellum) are discussed.

B1. ★Pop-up: Brain Lateralization

In this pop-up, the lateralized nature of the brain is discussed through a combination of text and graphics.

> **Brain Lateralization**
>
> **Type of Activity:** Illustrated Essay
>
> **Learning Objective:** Understand the lateralized nature of the brain and where this does and does not make a difference.

Faculty Note: In this illustrated essay, the lateralized nature of the brain is discussed. The topics that are covered include hemispheric dominance, hemispheric specialization, and communication between the two hemispheres. As with evolutionary accounts of gender differences, one of the dangers inherent in any discussion of lateralization is that students will overestimate the differences between the two hemispheres. There is often the tendency among students and the general public to assume that some behaviors, like creativity or logical reasoning, reside exclusively in one hemisphere or the other. This pop-up ends with a caution against making such conclusions. Most human behaviors are complex and likely involve many different areas in each of the brain's hemispheres. Whatever caused Mozart's musical genius, for example, or Marie Curie's intellectual prowess was not likely to have been confined to one hemisphere.

Additional Resources:
Split-brain.html—This site gives some of the history of split-brain surgery. It contains information, drawings, and links to other sites. http://www.indiana.edu/~pietsch/split-brain.html

C. The Midbrain
In this section the functions of the midbrain and reticular activating system are described.

D. The Forebrain
In this section, the functions of the various structures that make up the forebrain are described. These structures include the two cerebral hemispheres, the various lobes of the cortex, and the corpus callosum.

D1. ★Pop-up: The Interactive Brain
In this activity, students can explore the operation of various parts of the brain through a series of interactive animations and text.

The Interactive Brain

Type of Activity: Exploration
Learning Objective: Discover the functions that various anatomical structures in the brain perform.
Faculty Note: In this activity, students can click on the various structures in the brain and see animated descriptions of what each particular structure does. The animations are designed to be memorable and are intended to convey the gist of each structure's function.
Additional Resources:
A variety of sites containing images and models of brains can be found at:
The Whole Brain Atlas http://www.med.harvard.edu/AANLIB/home.html
3D MRI Rotation of the Human Head
http://www.ncsa.uiuc.edu/SDG/DigitalGallery/MRI_HEAD.html

D2. ★Pop-up: The Brain Structure and Function Game
In this activity, students can test their knowledge of the functions and locations of various brain structures.

The Brain Structure and Function Game

Type of Activity: Interactive Reinforcement
Learning Objective: Test students' mastery of the anatomy of the brain.
Faculty Note: In this activity, students can test their knowledge of the brain by dragging the names and functions of various structures in the brain to the appropriate locations on a drawing of the brain.

E. The Paradox of Plasticity

In this section, students are introduced to the notion of plasticity. One of psychology's great paradoxes is the fact that, while it is true that various parts of the brain serve specific functions, it is also true that these functions can migrate to other parts of the brain when the structure that typically regulates the function is damaged. In extreme cases, children have had one entire hemisphere surgically removed and suffered minimal loss of function.

Faculty Note: A brief case history highlighting plasticity and the mysteries of the brain can be found at http://www.indiana.edu/~pietsch/Lorber.html

F. Biological Causality Revisited

This unit ends by encouraging students to think critically about the relationship between biology of causality. While it is true that biology shapes psychological experience, the plastic nature of the brain also means that psychological experience shapes biology. Change the brain and you will likely change someone's psychological experience. Change psychological experience and you will likely change the brain.

Rapid Review 3

Quick Quiz

SENSATION TABLE OF CONTENTS

SENSATION
Annotated Outline

I. Introduction to Sensation
This unit begins with the distinction between sensation and perception.
A. Sensation and Perception

Sensation is defined as the raw experience of the stimulus. It occurs early in the sensation/perception cycle. Perception is defined as the final experience of an event or stimulus and the later steps the nervous system takes in interpreting that stimulus.

> **Faculty Note:** A classroom exercise that often helps with this distinction involves having students taste various items with and without the additional cues provided by smell. For example, under normal conditions 95% of the population can identify a single drop of coffee placed on the tongue. However, when smell is neutralized (e.g., when it is masked with a strong odor like camphor—the active ingredient in products like Vicks Vap-O-Rub or BenGay—only 3% of the population can correctly identify a drop of coffee (Mozell et al., 1969, Nasal chemoreception in flavor identification. <u>Archives of Otolaryngology</u>, <u>90</u>, 367-373). This difference suggests that taste (i.e., the sensations provided by the sensory receptors on the tongue) is a sensation, while flavor is a perception that involves combining taste, smell, texture, and temperature.

B. Bottom-Up and Top-Down Processing

In bottom-up processing, our perceptions are formed mainly from the data supplied by our sense organs. Relatively little interpretation is used to understand the stimuli we have observed. In top-down processing, our past experience and expectations influence our perceptual experience.

B1. ★Pop-up: Bottom-Up and Top-Down Processing

This pop-up provides a closer look at the distinction between bottom-up and top-down processing.

> ### Bottom-Up and Top-Down Processing
> **Activity Type:** Illustrated Essay
> **Learning Objective:** Introduce/Reinforce the distinction between Bottom-up and Top-Down Processing
> **Faculty Note:** Because the distinction between bottom-up and top-down processing is difficult for many students, this pop-up provides more details and examples of the difference and focuses on the interaction between the two processes.

C. How Many Senses Are There?

Students are reminded that psychologists study more than the traditional five senses. The senses identified on the disk also include equilibrium, kinesthesis, warmth, cold, and pain.

Faculty Note: Our students often raise questions about ESP in the context of discussions of the senses. The Pop-Up "Evaluating Evidence—Psychic Abilities" from the History and Methods section of this CD-ROM may be useful in this context. There, students are encouraged to think critically about investigations of ESP and the evidence that would be required to demonstrate its existence.

Rapid Review 1

II. Sensory Transduction

The idea of transduction is introduced by asking the age-old question, "If a tree fell in the woods and no one was around to hear it, would it still make a sound?" The position taken here is that, psychologically speaking, the answer is "no."

A. What Is Transduction?

All sensory systems confront the problem of transduction, defined here as the processes by which the physical properties of the stimulus are converted into electro-chemical signals that the nervous system can interpret.

B. Transduction and Odor

Transduction of odor is covered in this section.

Faculty Note: . Here, and later in the sensory coding and odor section, the popular "lock and key" model for olfaction is presented. According to this model, the shape of the molecule, determines which specific receptors are stimulated. The exact mechanisms of smell are still controversial and under intense investigation.

C. Transduction and Taste

Transduction of taste is covered in this section.

Faculty Note: You may notice that the traditional "areas of taste" on the tongue are not presented in the graphics on the CD. Recent research suggests that specific tastes are not localized on particular parts of the tongue. In fact, taste receptors are not confined to the tongue. They are located throughout the mouth and throat (Bartoshuk, L. M., [1993]. Genetic and pathological taste variation: What can we learn from animal models and human disease. In D. J. Chadwick, J. Marsh, & J. Good [Eds.], The Molecular Basis of Smell and Taste Transduction CIBA Foundation Symposia Series, No. 179, New York: Wylie.).

D. Transduction and Sound

Transduction of sound is covered in this section.

D1. ★Pop-up: Transduction and the Ear

The process of converting vibrations into neural messages is presented in the form of a narrated animation.

Transduction in the Ear

Type of Activity: Movie

Learning Objective: Understand the processes by which vibrations in the air are turned into neural signals.

Faculty Note: This animation provides a concrete visual presentation of the transduction in the ear. It covers transduction (i.e., getting the signal into the system), but not sensory coding. That is covered later in the CD under "Sensory Coding." If you decide to use these animations in your lecture, you may want to play the two movies sequentially.

D2. ★Ear Structure and Function

This activity allows students to explore the structures and functions of various parts of the ear.

Ear Structure and Function
Type of Activity: Interactive Reinforcement
Learning Objective: Learn and remember the functions of the major anatomical structures in the ear.
Faculty Note: In this activity, students can explore the anatomy of the ear by rolling their cursors over various structures in the ear and seeing their names and functions pop up. This information is later tested in the rapid review and a paper and pencil version of the activity is available in this guide. Also, because this section is concerned with the transduction of sound, there is no discussion of the functions of the semicircular canals. However, these structures are labeled in the interaction, in case you want to discuss the transduction of acceleration and movement.

E. Sensory Thresholds and Psychophysics

Defines psychophysics as the study of the relationship between the physical properties of a stimulus and the psychological experience of that stimulus.

E1. ★Pop-up: Psychophysics and Thresholds

Focuses on the psychophysical exploration of sensory limits. Both absolute and difference thresholds are defined.

Psychophysics and Thresholds
Type of Activity: Illustrated Essay
Learning Objective: Understand the difference between absolute thresholds and difference thresholds.
Faculty Note: This pop-up concentrates on thresholds and should go well with the "experiment in thresholds" activity that follows.

E2. ★Pop-up: An Experiment in Thresholds

Introduces the notion of the j.n.d. (just noticeable difference) and the idea that our psychological experiences of the world are shaped by the world, but do not correspond to the world in a one-to-one fashion.

An Experiment in Thresholds
Type of Activity: Simulation
Learning Objective: Understand the orderly relationship between physical stimulation and psychological experiences.
Faculty Note: In this simulation, students are introduced to the notion of the j.n.d. (just noticeable difference) and to the idea that our psychological experiences of the world are shaped by the world, but do not correspond to the world in a one-to-one fashion. To that end, students are given an opportunity to drag "virtual candles" into a dark room and observe changes in the perceived illumination of the room. What they should discover as they do the activity is that the number of candles needed to produce a j.n.d. increases as the ambient light increases. One question that may come up is whether the effects they see on their screen are "real." In fact, this activity simulates a psychophysical experiment. Because of inconsistencies in calibration and video processing across different computers, it is not possible to do a "real" psychophysical experiment of this type. Though not covered explicitly in the text, this activity may serve as an engaging springboard for discussing the contributions of specific psychophysicists including Weber, Fechner, and Stephens.

Rapid Review 2

III. Sensory Coding

A. What Is Sensory Coding?

Sensory coding is defined as the process of registering the intensity of a stimulus and the translation of its qualities into specific neural codes that the brain can interpret.

B. Coding and Odor

The underlying mechanisms responsible for identifying particular odors and their intensities are presented.

C. Coding and Sound

Explores the relationship between the physical properties of sound waves (i.e., frequency and amplitude) and the psychological experience of sound (i.e., pitch and volume).

C1. ★Pop-up: Coding in the Ear

This pop-up contains a narrated animation in which the place/frequency theory of pitch perception is presented.

Coding in the Ear
Type of Activity: Movie
Learning Objective: Understand sensory coding, in general, and the place/frequency theory of pitch perception specifically.
Faculty Note: This pop-up contains a narrated animation in which the place/frequency theory of pitch perception is presented. On a technical note, you may want to point out to your students that the depiction of the wave in the cochlea is simplified. In reality, the waves in the cochlea are "standing waves" (i.e., they form a fairly static pattern on the membrane) rather than traveling waves.
Additional Resources: This site contains a multimedia presentation of selected topics in auditory perception. It provides an interesting overview and includes lots of resources. Much of the site is fairly technical http://www.music.mcgill.ca/auditory/history.html

D. Coding and Sight

The processes involved in sensory coding are explored in relatively greater detail for the visual system than they are for the other senses.

D1. ★Eye Structure and Function

This activity allows students to explore the structures and functions of various parts of the eye.

Eye Structure and Function
Type of Activity: Interactive Reinforcement
Learning Objective: Learn and remember the functions of the major anatomical structures in the eye.
Faculty Note: In this activity, students can explore the anatomy of the eye by rolling their cursors over the various structures of the eye and seeing their names and functions pop up. This information is later tested in the rapid review and a paper and pencil version of the activity is available in this guide.

E. The Retina

The structure and functions of the retina are reviewed.

F. Electromagnetic Radiation

The relationships between electromagnetic radiation and "visible" light for humans and selected other species are reviewed.

G. Trichromatic Theory

How we perceive different colors is addressed through the trichromatic theory of color perception.

G1. ★Pop-up: Color Mixing
In this activity, students can mix colors both additively and subtractively.

Color Mixing
Type of Activity: Exploration
Learning Objective: Understand the differences between additive and subtractive color mixing; know which one is most relevant to how they eye mixes colors.
Faculty Note: In our experience, additive color mixing is one of the single most difficult concepts to get students to understand. Perhaps it is because most of their experience comes from coloring with crayons, but no matter how many times we ask students in lecture what green and red add to make, they answer brown (i.e., the subtractive mix). Because additive mixing more closely resembles the working of the visual system, this activity is included to help make the difference between subtractive and additive mixing concrete. In the activity, students can experiment with different combinations of additive and subtractive mixes and see what the results are. The activity also contains a movie that summarizes the additive and subtractive processes that are involved in looking at a yellow object.

G2. ★Pop-up: Defects in Color Perception
This activity simulates the experience of various forms of "color blindness."

Defects in Color Perception
Type of Activity: Interactive Animation
Learning Objective: Explore four types of color deficiency.
Faculty Note: This pop-up allows students to simulate the experience of various forms of "color blindness." If a student has persistent problems in discriminating between the various portrayals of color deficiency, she may want to have her vision checked by a professional.
Additional Resources:
Color Deficiency Test Page – This site, accessible from either of the URLs listed, contains information about color deficiency and includes the pseudoisochromatic plates used in testing color perception. http://www.cactus.org/~kingman/CVDtest.html
On a related front, http://www.lava.net/~dewilson/web/color.html is a web site devoted to the applied side of color perception and color deficiencies. Specifically, the site deals with issues of web site design as they affect people with color deficiencies. The site provides an overview of color deficiencies, personal anecdotes, and recommended design strategies.

H. Feature Detectors
Visual coding occurs both at the retina, through rods and cones, and in the brain via specialized neurons called feature detectors.

H1. ★Pop-up: A Nobel-Winning Study in Feature Detectors
Reviews the Nobel Prize winning research of Hubel and Wiesel through a combination of interactive animations and text.

A Nobel-Winning Study in Feature Detectors
Type of Activity: Illustrated Essay
Learning Objective: Review the discovery and importance of feature detectors.
Faculty Note: In this pop-up, the Nobel Prize winning research of Hubel and Wiesel is reviewed through a combination of interactive animations and text.

Rapid Review 3
IV. Sensory Adaptation
A. The Challenge of Adaptation
Sensory adaptation is presented as a common principle affecting all sensory systems.
B. Adapting to the Dark
Reviews the processes that occur when the eye adapts to the dark.
B1. ★Pop-up: Exploring Intensity
Students can explore the processes of adaptation to brightness through a pair of interactive demonstrations.

Exploring Intensity

Type of Activity: Exploration
Learning Objective: Experience and understand the processes involved in sensory adaptation.
Faculty Note: In this activity, students explore the processes of adaptation to brightness through a pair of interactions. One interaction is done in color while the other is done in black and white. In each, students are asked to stare at the computer screen. While they stare at the screen, they see an image in which one side is blue (color version) or gray (black and white version) and the other side is black. After approximately 20 seconds (though it will probably seem longer), these images are replaced by a single uniformly colored image. However, because of adaptation, these images should briefly appear to be made up of two different shades of blue (color version) or gray (black and white version).
You may want to point out to your students that this activity has everything to do with brightness and little to do with color. In both the color and black and white versions, the adaptation is to the intensity of the stimulus, not to its hue.

C. Color Afterimages
This section introduces afterimages, generally, and explains color afterimages, specifically, in terms of opponent processes in the visual system.
C1. ★Pop-up: Creating Color Afterimages
Students can experience and explore afterimages by creating their own color combinations and seeing what happens when they adapt to them.

Creating Color Afterimages

Type of Activity: Exploration
Learning Objective: Understand how opponent processes and sensory adaptation contribute to the experience of afterimages.
Faculty Note: In this activity, students can create their own stimuli for creating color afterimages. A few of tips for this activity:
First, color afterimages tend to be robust. It is the rare student who does not experience color afterimage.
Second, if you have access to a digital projector, this activity works well as a lecture demonstration.
Third, color afterimages can also be used to demonstrate the constructed nature of depth perception (see the section on the Ponzo illusion on the CD). Specifically, if students adapt to the color afterimage stimulus, and then stare at a neutral wall, rather than at the computer screen, the afterimage should resize and appear much larger. This resizing happens because the retinal afterimage remains constant in size, but depth cues lead the brain to conclude that it has moved further away and must, therefore, be bigger.

D. Motion Afterimages

Motion afterimages are introduced and discussed in terms of opponent processes among feature detectors in the visual cortex.

D1. ★Pop-up: Experiencing Motion Afterimages

Students can experience and explore motion afterimages.

Experiencing Motion Afterimages
Type of Activity: Exploration
Learning Objective: Understand how opponent processes and feature detectors contribute to the experience of motion afterimages.
Faculty Note: In this activity, students are given an opportunity to stare at a rotating spiral image. This should lead to adaptation of inward feature detectors in the visual cortex. After approximately 20 seconds, the rotating spiral is replaced by a stationary drawing of an eye. However, because of the adaptation of the inward feature detectors, the eye should look like it is expanding (i.e., moving out). The accompanying text explains why this occurs.
One word of caution, unlike color afterimages, motion afterimages are fragile and happen very quickly. If your students don't experience the motion afterimage, they might want to try again, holding their heads as still as possible during the adaptation and test phases.

What Do We Learn From Afterimages?

In this section, the processes involved in color and motion afterimages are briefly reviewed.

E1. ★Pop-up: In the Head or in the Eye?

In this activity, students can compare color and motion afterimage effects and discover that color afterimages happen close to the retina, while the motion afterimages happen in the visual cortex.

In the Head or in the Eye?
Type of Activity: Exploration
Learning Objective: Experience and understand some of the differences between cortical and retinal processing.
Faculty Note: In this activity, students are encouraged to experiment further with color and motion afterimages. Specifically, the instructions for the activity ask them to try the adaptation activities again. This time, however, they are instructed to cover one eye during the adaptation phase of the activity and observe their experiences in the adapted and unadapted eyes. What the students should discover is that while color afterimages are experienced only in the adapted eye, motion afterimages can be experienced with either eye. The adaptation that occurs with color happens close to the retina, while the adaptation that occurs with motion happens in the visual cortex.

Rapid Review 4
Quick Quiz

PERCEPTION TABLE OF CONTENTS

PERCEPTION
Annotated Outline
I. INTRODUCTION TO PERCEPTION

A. From Sensation to Perception

The metaphor of an artist is used to illustrate some of the differences between sensation and perception. Like an artist who uses the oils and canvas to create a painting that is more than the sum of its parts, perception relies upon the integration of many separate pieces of information.

Faculty Note: One of the more ambitious projects on the web is a "web book" by Peter K. Kaiser. Entitled "The Joy of Visual Perception" this site/book combines hyperlinking and interactivity to present an overview of visual perception. It contains lots of graphics and examples, though the writing is fairly technical. http://www.yorku.ca/eye/

B. Gestalt Psychology and Perceptual Laws

The Gestalt perspective is introduced through two activities: an interactive sound clip and animations of selected Gestalt Principles.

B1. ★Perceiving Sound

Students can listen to an audio clip that contains two versions of the song "Twinkle, Twinkle, Little Star." Despite significant differences between the two versions, students will "hear" the same song because they will impose organization on the stimulus—the essence of the Gestalt position.

Perceiving Sound

Type of Activity: Audio Demonstration

Learning Objective: Demonstrate that perception involves imposing order on the stimulus. Make concrete the Gestalt Dictum that maintains that the perceptual whole is greater than the sum of its parts.

Faculty Note: This audio clip contains two versions of the song "Twinkle, Twinkle, Little Star." Despite significant differences between the two versions (e.g., different pace and complexity), students will "hear" the same song. This effect highlights the fact that we often impose organization on the stimulus—the essence of the Gestalt position.

B2. ★Exploring Gestalt Principles

Animations are used to illustrate the gestalt principles of proximity, closure, similarity, and continuity.

51

Exploring Gestalt Principles

Activity Type: Interactive Animation

Learning Objective: Understand basic Gestalt Principles.

Faculty Note: This activity includes animations that illustrate the gestalt principles of proximity, closure, similarity, and continuity.

Additional Resources:

One of the easiest ways to see Gestalt Principles in action is to look at how they emerge in art. An interesting web site that tackles this issue can be found at http://www.brad.ac.uk/acad/optom/SPTut/art/index.html

II. PERCEPTUAL CONSTANCY

Perceptual constancies are introduced to reinforce, again, the distinction between sensation and perception. Our sensory experiences frequently change (e.g., the light dims, the image on the retina gets smaller) but our perceptions often remain the same.

II1. ★Illustrations of Visual Constancy

This pop-up allows students to explore color, size, and shape constancy through a series of animations.

Illustration of Visual Constancy

Type of Activity: Interactive Animation

Learning Objective: Understand Shape Constancy.

Faculty Note: The goal of this activity is to help students see how changes in the orientation of an object lead to dramatic changes in the shape of an image that is cast on the retina. Nevertheless, our perception of the object remains constant. To that end, the activity includes two animations that show a door opening and closing. One animation depicts the door in all its rendered glory. The other depicts the door in outline form as it would appear on the flat surface of the retina. As students play and pause the animations, they should get some idea about how the retinal shape of the image changes as the door's orientation varies.

II2. ★Illustrations of Other Visual Constancy

In this section, students can continue to explore a variety of visual constancies.

+---+
| **Illustrations of Other Visual Constancies** |
| |
| **Type of Activity:** Interactive Animation |
| |
| **Learning Objective:** Understand shape, size, and color constancies |
| and what they tell us about the constructed nature of perception. |
| |
| **Faculty Note:** We have found that students often lose sight of the |
| critical points in illustrations like these. In all of these |
| animations, the primary point is not that the stimulus doesn't |
| change—it does. Instead, the point is that the general perception |
| does not change. For example, when the illumination changes on the |
| bananas contained in the color constancy animation, their appearance |
| does change. But they would still be described as "yellow." Similarly,|
| the image size of the cow in the size constancy animation does change |
| as it is hurled into the distance. But the cow is not assumed to be |
| getting smaller, just further away. It's perceived size is constant. |
| (BTW, no cows were harmed in the making of this CD!) |
+---+

Rapid Review 1

III. PERCEPTIONS AS DECISIONS

In this section, perceptions are presented as decisions that depend both upon the stimulus and the response criteria of the perceiver. Specifically, signal detection theory, with its emphasis on detectability and response bias, is introduced.

A. Signal Detection Theory

Signal detection theory is introduced.

B. Response Bias

The notion that our responses depend, in part, upon our decision criteria is introduced.

C. The Case of the USS Vincennes

The 1988 downing of an Iranian jetliner is presented as a case study in signal detection theory.

D. Detection and Decision

Continuing the Vincennes example, this section emphasizes how the simple act of saying "I saw something" is not an automatic response, but rather the culmination of a decision process that depends upon more than the mere presence of a signal.

E. Hits and Misses

In this section, hits, misses, false alarms, and correct rejections are defined.

F. Types of Errors

This section focuses on the relationship between accuracy and response bias under conditions of marginal detectability.

F1. ★Pop-up: A Simulation of Signal Detection

This activity allows students to participate in a signal detection task under two different decision criteria. After completing the two sets of judgments, the students see how they did and learn more about Type I and Type II errors.

A Simulation of Signal Detection

Type of Activity: Simulation

Learning Objective: Understand the key elements of signal detection theory including decision criteria, response bias, detectability, and Type I and Type II errors.

Faculty Note: In this activity, students are encouraged to imagine that they are radar operators on a military ship. Their task is to watch a radar screen and decide whether they "see" an enemy missile on each sweep of the radar. On the first set of eight trials, they are urged to be absolutely sure that they have seen an enemy missile before issuing an alarm. On the second set of eight trials, they are encouraged to sound the alarm if they think it is at all possible that they saw a missile. After completing the two sets of judgments, the students can see how they did. What students should discover from this activity is that their accuracy (i.e., the number of hits + correct rejections) was the same across the two kinds of judgment. What varies is the kind of errors they make. When urged to be cautious about sounding the alarm, students should frequently miss the missiles that were there (a.k.a., Type II error) but have few false alarms (a.k.a., Type I errors). In contrast, when instructed to sound the alarm at the slightest provocation, they should have relatively few misses and many false alarms.

To more dramatically illustrate the main points about response biases, students may also be encouraged to run through this exercise again. The second time through they can answer "Yes" to every question about the enemy missile, ultimately seeing the elimination of any dangerous "misses" but with the much greater cost in expensive false alarms. Conversely, answering "No" to all queries about the presence of the missiles will let all of them through their defenses (many misses), but no friendlies will be shot down (no false alarms). The trade-off in types of potential errors may be more vividly illustrated in this fashion.

Although the difficulty of the simulated radar detection task is intended to be identical with both sets of instructions, there may be a slight practice effect as students gain experience with the task. In other words, their total error rate may drop slightly during the second set of radar sweeps. The main point remains the same, however. The most significant change should be in the shift from misses to false alarms as the primary type of error made by the student.

You may want to continue discussion of the principles of signal detection theory in other (nonmilitary) contexts:

- When airport metal detectors are tuned to their maximum sensitivity in the aftermath of a publicized act of terrorism, the increased chance of correctly detecting a terrorist's weapon (a "hit") is accompanied by an irritating increase in the number of false alarms for watches, keys, and belt buckles.

- When scientists test hypotheses, the type of error that they are most concerned about is making a false claim of a significant finding when, in fact, the evidence doesn't support it. Responsible researchers should maintain a response bias that allows them to control any tendencies towards false alarms (Type I errors) while still having a reasonable chance of discovering something interesting. One of the reasons that inferential statistics are employed by scientists is to allow them to control these types of errors. (A classic example here is the case of the apparent discovery of "cold fusion" by chemists at the University of Utah. These researchers held press conferences claiming a dramatic and unexpected discovery of "nuclear fusion in a test tube" but in their enthusiasm had actually misinterpreted some ambiguous evidence in their experiments).

- Our judicial system is intended to balance various types of errors in making legal decisions. Jury members in a criminal trial are faced with what amounts to a signal detection task, making a decision about a defendant's guilt under conditions of uncertainty. Evidentiary rules (such as Miranda rights) are intended to produce a response bias that will minimize false alarms (convicting an innocent person), although critics sometimes bemoan the tradeoff in increased "misses" (guilty defendants set free on technicalities).

Rapid Review 2

G. How Do We Perceive Depth?

In this section, binocular and monocular depth cues are introduced as tools that perceivers use to construct a three dimensional perception from a two dimensional retinal image.

G1. ★Pop-up: Types of Depth Cues

In this pop-up, students are encouraged to explore a variety of monocular and binocular depth cues.

Types of Depth Cues

Activity Type: Interactive Animation

Learning Objective: Understand binocular and monocular depth cues.

Faculty Note: In this activity, students can click on the names of various depth cues and see how they are manifested in a photograph.

H. How Do We Perceive Motion?

This section raises the question of how we move from an erratic, constantly changing retinal image to a perception of smooth and continuous motion.

I. Direct Perception of Motion

Direct perception theories argue that all of the information needed to perceive motion is contained in the stimulus itself. An animation depicting "optic flow" is used to illustrate this point.

> **Faculty Note:** In this CD-ROM (and in many textbooks) a great deal of attention is devoted to theories of motion perception that assume the individual is "constructing" an impression of movement based on inference and experience. A useful counterpoint is the direct perception theory of motion perception, originally articulated by Gibson, that assumes that it is a "bottom up" process that requires little in the way of inference or decisions on the part of the perceiver. Moving stimuli activate feature detectors in the brain, which directly responds to that pattern of stimulation by generating a subjective experience of movement. Recent discoveries of feature detectors intended to detect motion in particular directions, especially the "looming" movements of objects towards the perceiver, tend to lend credence to this model.

I1. ★Perception of Motion Movie

This movie begins with a static image that appears to be of randomly placed dots on a gray background. Once the image is set in motion, it becomes clear that the movie is of a man climbing a stepladder. Presumably, this information becomes available directly from the moving stimulus, not through the addition of context or cues.

> ### Perception of Motion Movie
>
> **Type of Activity:** Movie
>
> **Learning Objective:** Encourage students to think critically about direct versus constructed theories of perception..
>
> **Faculty Note:** To further illustrate the direct perception perspective, students are first presented with a static image that appears to be of randomly placed dots on a gray background. It could be a picture of almost anything. Once the image is set in motion, however, it becomes clear that the movie is of a man climbing a stepladder. The point of the movie is that all of the information becomes available directly from the moving stimulus, not through the addition of context or cues.
>
> **Additional Resources:**
>
> More information on the direct perception approach can be found at the International Society for Ecological Society web site at http://www.trincoll.edu/~psyc/isep.html

J. Constructed Perception of Motion

Constructed theories of motion perception argue that we actively combine many sources of information to infer that a stimulus is moving.

J1. ★Pop-up: Apparent Motion—The Phi Phenomenon

In this pop-up, students can examine the effects that various presentation rates have on the perception of motion via the phi phenomenon (a.k.a., stroboscopic motion).

Apparent Motion—The Phi Phenomenon

Type of Activity: Exploration

Learning Objective: Become familiar with the phi phenomenon and understand the implications it has for our understanding of motion perception.

Faculty Note: In this activity, students can explore the effects that various rates of presentation have on the phi phenomenon. The question of how the brain fuses the images together remains one of the great, unanswered questions in vision research.

Rapid Review 3

IV. PERCEPTUAL ILLUSIONS

The final section of the perception unit focuses on illusions—instances in which the subjective experience of a stimulus does not match its objective characteristics.

Faculty Note: "Illusion galleries" are proliferating on the web. Two of the better galleries are http://www.illusionworks.com and http://valley.uml.edu/landrigan/illusion.html. The Illusion Works site, in particular, has very nice demonstrations and fairly accessible explanations.

A. Bottom-Up Illusions

This section introduces bottom-up illusions. In bottom-up illusions, the illusions occur because of the ways in which our sensory systems are physiologically wired.

A1. ★Pop-up: The Twisted Cords Illusion

In this illusion, students can control the orientations of slanted lines that overwhelm the feature detectors in the visual cortex and cause the illusion to occur.

The Twisted Cords Illusion

Type of Activity: Exploration

Learning Objective: Understand feature detectors and the role that they play in the occurrence of the twisted cords illusion.

Faculty Note: In this activity, students can control the presence and orientation of angled lines that give rise to the twisted cords illusion. The illusion occurs because the many slanted lines comprising the "cords" over stimulate feature detectors that react specifically to lines of just that orientation. Presumably this stimulation overwhelms and distorts the perceived orientation of the larger vertical lines. Students can verify this explanation by exploring what happens as they change and remove the angled lines.

A2. ★Pop-up: The Hermann Grid Illusion

In this illusion, students can examine the effects of changing the size of the intersections in the Hermann Grid.

The Hermann Grid

Type of Activity: Exploration

Learning Objective: Demonstrate lateral inhibition.

Faculty Note: The Herman Grid illustrates the effects of lateral inhibition in the neural substrate of the eye. Receptors responding to the white intersections of the grid are relatively more inhibited by neighboring receptors (which are active due to the bright areas around the intersections). This creates "gray" splotches of lesser brightness at those intersections. In this activity, students can control the size of the intersections in the Hermann Grid and examine the subsequent changes in the experience of the illusion.

Additional Resources:

More information on the receptive fields of the retina and the principles of lateral inhibition which produce these effects can be found at:
http://psych.hanover.edu/Krantz/receptive/index.html. In addition to general information about perception, this site contains an entire interactive tutorial devoted to the topic of receptive fields.

B. Top-Down Illusions

Top-down illusions occur when our assumptions, preconceptions, and past experience distort our interpretation of the objective properties of the stimulus.

B1. ★Pop-up: The Ponzo Illusion

In this illusion, students can examine the effects that adding and removing depth cues have on the Ponzo Illusion (a.k.a. the "running monsters" illusion).

> **The Ponzo Illusion**
>
> **Activity Type:** Exploration
>
> **Learning Objective:** Understand how depth cues contribute to the Ponzo Illusion.
>
> **Faculty Note:** The Ponzo illusion occurs when one image subjectively appears larger than another, despite the fact that there is no objective difference in size. In this activity, students can control the presence of depth cues in the Ponzo illusion. When the depth cues are present (i.e., linear perspective, height in the scene), one image is perceived to be farther away than the other. Given that both images are the same size, the brain interprets the more distant image as larger. It is this inferential process that creates the illusory size differences.
>
> The Ponzo Illusion can also be used as a starting point for a discussion of the moon illusion. Though multiple explanations for the moon illusion exist, depth cues clearly play a role. To demonstrate this role, you need an evening when the moon looks unusually large and a tube from a roll of paper towels. First look at the moon with the naked eye and then look at it through the tube. Because the tube blocks out the depth cues found on the horizon, the illusion should diminish.

B2. ★Pop-up: The Ambiguous Woman Illusion

In this illusion, students can see various interpretations of an ambiguous figure highlighted.

> **The Ambiguous Woman Illusion**
>
> **Activity Type:** Demonstration
>
> **Learning Objective:** Recognize the role that expectations and perceptual sets play in our interpretations of objects.
>
> **Faculty Note:** This activity allows students to look at a version of the ambiguous young woman/old woman that has been around since the early 1900s. The original figure is from an advertising campaign. Students can look at the ambiguous figure or with the features that lead to each interpretation highlighted. The text focuses on the role that expectations play in determining how ambiguous stimuli are perceived.

B3. ★Pop-up: The Reversible Figure Illusion

The face-vase illusion illustrates the Gestalt notions of "figure" and "ground," with students having control over what appears as figure or ground.

> **The Reversible Figure Illusion**
>
> **Activity Type:** Demonstration
>
> **Learning Objective:** Explore the Gestalt notion of Figure/Ground.

Rapid Review 4

Quick Quiz

LEARNING AND MEMORY TABLE OF CONTENTS

LEARNING AND MEMORY
Annotated Outline

I. INTRODUCTION TO LEARNING

Learning is introduced and described as any change in behavior that is a result of experience. Any organism with a nervous system, from the simplest invertebrates to human beings, is capable of learning from experience.

II. LEARNING THROUGH ASSOCIATION: CLASSICAL CONDITIONING

Classical conditioning is discussed as a type of associative learning. The initial investigations of this form of learning were conducted by the Russian physiologist Ivan Pavlov at the turn of the century, using dogs as subjects.

II1. ★Pop-Up: A Profile of Ivan Pavlov

A brief biographical sketch of Ivan Pavlov is provided, beginning with his early days as a student and continuing through his contributions to the description of classical conditioning.

> ### A Profile of Ivan Pavlov
>
> **Activity Type:** Illustrated Essay
>
> **Learning Objective:** Learn about Pavlov's early life and professional work in psychology.
>
> **Faculty Note:** The intent of this biographical sketch is to personalize and perhaps humanize an historical figure in psychology that some students regard as distant and quaint.
>
> **Additional Resources:**
>
> The first account of Pavlov's work to appear in the United States was published by R. M. Yerkes and S. Morgulis in 1909. The text of that account can be found at http://www.yorku.ca/dept/psych/classics/Yerkes/pavlov.htm

A. What Is Conditioning?

Conditioning is said to occur when a previously neutral stimulus acquires the power to elicit simple reflexes in an organism.

B. A Three-Step Process

Conditioned responses are described as being acquired in a three-step process. In the first step, an unconditioned stimulus naturally evokes an unconditioned response. In the second step, a neutral stimulus is paired repeatedly with the unconditioned stimulus. In the third step, the previously neutral stimulus (now called the conditioned stimulus) now has the ability to evoke the conditioned response.

C. Later Work in Classical Conditioning

The process of extinction is described as the gradual breakdown of conditioned associations. Extinguished responses are rarely eliminated entirely, and may be relearned easily.

C1. ★Pop-Up: The Classical Conditioning Matching Game

Here we provide a drag-and-drop activity in which students classify the critical elements of five different learning situations.

The Classical Conditioning Matching Game

Type of Activity: Interactive Reinforcement

Learning Objective: Provide students with an opportunity to test their knowledge of the UCS, UCR, CS, and CR and to apply that knowledge to new situations.

Faculty Note: In this activity, students can test their knowledge of classical conditioning by reading scenarios and dragging the highlighted stimuli and responses to their appropriate labels (e.g., In Pavlov's studies, **meat powder** was the **UCS**).

This type of activity can be repeated in the classroom, once students get familiar with the one presented. New conditioning scenarios that are topical or tailored for the class can be introduced and students can identify the UCS, UCR, CS, and CR in the new descriptions.

Additional Resources:

A host of other conditioning examples can be found at http://www.sfu.ca/~tbauslau/302/cc.html

---

D. Conditioned Phobias

Conditioning is argued to be an explanation of some phobias (intense, irrational fears). John B. Watson is credited with an early application of Pavlov's principles of classical conditioning to the learning of emotional reactions.

D1. ★Pop-Up: A Profile of John Watson

A brief biographical sketch of John Watson is provided here, beginning with his early days as a student and describing some of the professional and personal controversies in which he was involved.

E. The Case of Little Albert

A brief account of the infamous "Little Albert" study is provided here. In this study John B. Watson and a research assistant named Rosalie Rayner attempted to condition a simple fear of rats in an 11-month-old infant. The conditioned fear was later found to have generalized to other similar stimuli. The study is noted to be ethically controversial.

E1. ★Archival Footage of Little Albert

Here we see actual film footage of "Little Albert," John Watson, Rosalie Rayner and the rat.

E2. ★Pop-Up: Conditioning and Drug Addiction

Classical conditioning of drug tolerance in rats and humans is described. Conditioning helps to explain an unusual finding: among heroin users who end up in emergency rooms with the symptoms of a heroin overdose, most (about 70 percent) have apparently not taken more than their usual dose.

Conditioning and Drug Addiction

Activity Type: Illustrated Essay

Learning Objective: Help students see applications of learning theory to life outside the laboratory.

Faculty Note: This example uses the traditional pedagogical technique of presenting a puzzle or counter-intuitive finding that can be explained by the principle under consideration. In this case, it's the observation that 70% of heroin overdose cases seen in the ER don't actually involve a true "overdose" of the drug. Classical conditioning of tolerance or autonomic "opposition" to the drug in response to particular circumstances may help explain this effect.

It may be worth noting that it is possible to classically condition not only overt responses (observable behaviors), but also autonomic responses, such as drug tolerance and even immune system responses.

Additional Resources:

An electronic slide show of Seigel's 1975 study of conditioned drug tolerance can be found at http://www.personal.kent.edu/~dwallac1/Classic/ppframe.htm

---

F. Watson and Behaviorism

Watson was convinced that conditioning accounted for not only unusual emotional responses such as phobias and fetishes, but could provide an explanation of most human learning. Conditioning theory was also consistent with the goal of behaviorism, which was to explain behavior without referring to unseen mental processes.

G. Instrumental Learning

In this section, the more active process of instrumental learning is introduced. The pioneering psychologist E.L. Thorndike first articulated the notion that behaviors are shaped by their consequences, a principle known as the "law of effect."

G1. ★Pop-Up: A Profile of E.L. Thorndike

A brief biographical sketch of E.L. Thorndike is provided here, including his early work with animal learning (the "puzzle box" studies) which led to his statement of the law of effect. His later work in educational psychology is also described.

A Profile of E.L. Thorndike

Activity Type: Illustrated Essay

Learning Objective: Learn about Thorndike's life and his progression from studies of animal learning to his more applied work with human learning and education.

Faculty Note: Thorndike's life presents an interesting spectrum of interests and a fascinating career track in psychology.

He began his career as a comparative psychologist studying learning in cats. It may be appropriate to note that a critical difference between a psychologist who studies animal behavior and researchers from other disciplines who study animal behavior (such as zoologists or ethologists) is that psychologists will, by definition, eventually attempt to apply their findings to human behavior. Such was the case with Thorndike.

Skinner's more elaborate operant conditioning theory is the direct descendant of Thorndike's simple "Law of Effect."

Rapid Review 1

III. LEARNING FROM CONSEQUENCES: OPERANT CONDITIONING

B.F. Skinner described the role of positive reinforcement, negative reinforcement, and punishment in shaping behavior, a process that he called operant conditioning.

III1. ★Pop-Up: A Profile of B.F. Skinner

A brief biographical sketch of B.F. Skinner is provided here, including his early days as a struggling writer, his chaotic graduate school program, and his development of the technology of behavior modification.

A Profile of B. F. Skinner

Activity Type: Illustrated Essay

Learning Objective: Learn about Skinner's life, work, and extensive advocacy of behaviorist principles.

A. Reinforcement

Positive reinforcement is described in this section as a rewarding consequence that encourages a behavior. Negative reinforcement is described as the process of encouraging a behavior that enables you to avoid or reduce an undesirable consequence.

B. Punishment

Punishment is described as any consequence that decreases the probability of a behavior being repeated.

B1. ★Pop-Up: Types of Reinforcement in Humans

Here the distinction is made between primary reinforcers that are based on biological needs (such as food or water) and secondary reinforcers that are learned by association (such as money or praise).

B2. ★Pop-Up: The Consequences Matching Game

Illustrative examples of positive reinforcers, negative reinforcers, and punishments are provided, and the student is asked to correctly classify each example.

The Consequences Matching Game

Activity Type: Interactive Reinforcement

Learning Objective: Provide students with a chance to test their knowledge of reinforcers and their ability to apply that knowledge to new situations.

Faculty Note: Many students find the distinctions among positive reinforcement, negative reinforcement, and punishment confusing. In this activity, their task is to identify and match examples of each of these concepts to the appropriate label by "dragging" it with the mouse. (So, the example, "A cookie for cleaning your room," would be correctly labeled as an instance of positive reinforcement.)

While most of the examples are straightforward and easy to label, there may be some categorizations that will provoke discussion. It may also be useful to come up with additional examples for class that are more difficult to categorize. For example, when a convict gets "time off for good behavior," is the good behavior being positively reinforced by the prospect of freedom, or is the good behavior being negatively reinforced by the avoidance of unpleasant jail time?

Additional Resources:

Additional examples can be found at http://server.bmod.athabascau.ca/html/prtut/reinpair.htm

http://www.sfu.ca/~tbauslau/302/rp.html

B3. ★Skinner Speaks

A film clip of Skinner himself describing the basic elements of operant conditioning, using a pigeon and a Skinner box as part of the demonstration is included.

C. How the Environment Shapes Behavior

Operant conditioning is said to shape behavior through a gradual process of trial and error. Even apparently complex behaviors can be built up over time from simpler ones.

D. The Interaction Between Classical and Operant Conditioning

Both classical and operant conditioning principles are sometimes necessary to account for complex behavior. In the case of a phobia, the initial fear may be classically conditioned but the later avoidance of the stimulus is a product of operant conditioning.

D1. ★Little Albert, Hollywood Style

A "silent-film" style movie recounting of the classical conditioning of a simple phobia and the operant conditioning that helps perpetuate such fears.

tendency to learn to avoid unpleasant stimuli (negative reinforcement) means that we never give ourselves the opportunity to unlearn these responses.

The notion that a given behavior can be influenced by multiple factors, including more than one type of learning, is noteworthy.

Rapid Review 2

IV. OPENING THE BLACK BOX: COGNITIVE LEARNING

Extreme or "radical" behaviorism is described as giving way to mounting evidence that other factors (e.g., cognition and mental representation) are important in the learning process.

IV1. ★Pop-Up: A Demonstration of the Black Box vs. the Mind

Cognitive psychologists believe that behavior cannot be understood without taking into account internal mental processes. As students search for the solution to the puzzle in this activity, they should reflect on the mental processes and specific strategies used to solve the problem.

A Demonstration of the Black Box vs. the Mind

Activity Type: Simulation

Learning Objective: Help students subjectively understand the difference between behavioristic and cognitive accounts of behavior.

Faculty Note: Radical behaviorists argued that psychology should try to explain behavior without making reference to any unseen mental process. In contrast, cognitive psychologists believe that behavior cannot be understood without taking into account internal mental processes such as plans, schemas, and mental images.

The task for the student is to play a game in which they have to find a correct combination of settings that will solve a puzzle. After searching for the correct setting, students are asked about their attempts. Did they try different solutions at random (trial-and-error) or did they employ some sort of cognitive strategy?

Is it possible to give a convincing account of the student's problem-solving behavior without exploring their mental representations of the problem?

A. The Problem of Biological Preparedness

The example of conditioned taste aversion in rats is used to illustrate the idea that some responses are more easily conditioned than others, perhaps because the organism is biologically "prepared" to learn them. Biological preparedness is presented as a challenge to radical behaviorism.

B. The Problem of Language

It is observed that the ease with which humans acquire language skills is a problem for behaviorism. It is particularly difficult to account for our learning of the syntax (rules) of language solely by trial-and-error learning.

C. The Problem of Social Learning

Here it is noted that the ability to learn vicariously (through observation of others) is yet a third problem for radical behaviorism. In a powerful demonstration of social learning, Albert Bandura and his colleagues found that children imitate the aggressive behaviors of an adult model.

C1. ★Archival Footage of the Bandura Study

In this footage from a classic study of the social learning of aggression, episodes of modeling are illustrated with clips of the adult model and the subsequent behavior of the children.

Archival Footage of the Bandura Study

Activity Type: Movie

Learning Objective: Provide an opportunity for students to see footage from a classic study that demonstrated the power of social learning.

Faculty Note: In this footage we see (and hear Bandura describing) the actions of an adult modeling aggressive behaviors, as well as the subsequent aggressive behaviors of a child in the study. The narration points out instances of direct imitation on the part of the child.

Not only does this illustrate actual subject behavior from an influential study of social learning, but it can be tied into a discussion of methodological choices, as well. Bandura's study was notable for being one of the earlier experimental studies of the impact of observational learning on aggression, but there are other ways of addressing this question, such as looking for correlations between exposure to violent TV programming and aggressive behavior.

Additional Resources:

A brief biography of Albert Bandura's can be found at
http://www.ship.edu/~cgboeree/bandura.html

D. The Problem of Representation

It is observed in this section that the final challenge to the views of radical behaviorists came in the form of an increasing interest in cognitive psychology. Studies of mental representation and imagery revealed that actions performed on mental images in many ways resemble those that we perform on objects in the real world. Roger Shepard's studies of mental rotation are cited as examples of this cognitive revolution.

D1. ★Pop-Up: An Experiment in Mental Rotation

In this activity, students will get an opportunity to visualize and mentally rotate selected images in a simple simulation of an experiment in cognitive psychology. Roger Shepard's original study revealed that his subjects were constructing mental models of the objects that were similar to their real-world counterparts.

An Experiment in Mental Rotation

Activity Type: Simulation

Learning Objective: Provide a concrete example of what it means to say that there is a mental representation of something and that that representation matters for behavior.

Faculty Note: In a simulated Shepard mental rotation task, students see two geometric figures in different rotations and are asked to decide whether the figures match. The time that it takes them to make these decisions and their subjective perceptions of how difficult each trial is will be recorded.

In the original study, Shepard found that the time it took subjects to decide whether the objects matched was predictable from the difference in their orientations. It was as if his subjects mentally rotated images of these objects just as they would have rotated real objects to determine if they matched. This illustrates a classic finding of the cognitive revolution, that although no one has ever "seen" a mental model of a physical object, their existence can be inferred from actual behaviors such as reaction times or judgments. Unseen mental events may be scientifically studied by inferences made from observable events.

Rapid Review 3

V. INTRODUCTION TO MEMORY

It is pointed out that the processes involved in memory are much more active, interpretive, and open to bias than we would like to believe. Memory is not simply a straightforward "recording" of events.

V1. ★A Test of Memory I

Students often fail to recognize the image of a commonly seen object (a real penny) when presented with many slightly different distracters. This is used to dramatize the limitations of memory.

A. Ebbinghaus and the Process of Forgetting

Hermann Ebbinghaus was the first psychologist to systematically study memory. Based on tests of his own memory, he was able to quantify remembering and forgetting, and evolve a model of memory based on the principle of association.

B. The Problem of Meaning

Although Ebbinghaus intentionally studied memory for "meaningless" information (such as nonsense syllables), it is well established that memories for material that is meaningful to us are more easily created and retrieved. This departs from a simple association model of memory.

B1. ★A Test of Memory II

A narrated description of "Washing Clothes" is used to illustrate the importance of meaningfulness in the encoding of new memories.

contrasted with memory for the same passage once it is given new meaning by the label "Washing Clothes."

Early models of memory based only on the principle of association (such as that of Ebbinghaus) fail to explain the impact of meaning on memory.

Additional Resources:

Ebbinghaus' *Memory: A Contribution to Experimental Psychology* can be found at http://www.yorku.ca/dept/psych/classics/Ebbinghaus/index.htm

C. Information Processing and Memory

Examples like the Washing Clothes exercise described above demonstrate that there is more to memory than simple associations. Information is actively processed and infused with meaning.

VI. The Memory Process

In theories of memory that emphasize information processing, it is often found to be useful to look at memory as if it occurs in three stages: encoding, storage, and retrieval.

A. Stage 1: Memory Encoding

Information to be remembered first has to be brought into the system. Selective attention is the most important principle governing this encoding process.

A1. ★A Test of Memory III

A complex video clip first used by the cognitive psychologist Ulrich Neisser provides an illustration of the role of selective attention in the encoding of memories. Students "filter out" elements of the action in the video when they are attending to other stimuli.

A Test of Memory III

Activity Type: Demonstration

Learning Objective: Learn about the role that selective attention plays in memory.

Faculty Note: This is a demonstration of selective attention that is constructed from a presentation of Neisser's classic video. The video begins with 4 people bouncing a basketball back and forth. Several men play basketball in a confusing montage of overlapping images. At one point during the video, a woman with an umbrella strolls by in the midst of the activity. After watching the video, the students will be asked to recall details from the game and player characteristics. In addition, they will be asked about the presence of the woman. Neisser found that the majority of people, selectively intent on watching the game, fail to see the woman.

Attention is a central mechanism in the formation of memories. One reason why we might find ourselves unable to retrieve information is that it was never really stored in the first place. We selectively attend to and encode only a fraction of the "booming, buzzing" confusion of events in the world around us, and so our allocation of attention "filters out" a substantial number of events that are thus "lost."

B. Stage 2: Memory Storage

For memory to function, information must be retained or stored over time. Psychologists have identified three steps that are involved in storing memories: sensory memory, short-term memory, and long-term memory.

C. Sensory Memory Storage

Sensory memory is described as a memory register that briefly preserves a faithful copy of incoming sensory information. George Sperling's classic studies of the duration and capacity of sensory memory are described in this section.

D. Short-Term Memory Storage

Short–term memory is described here as "working" memory, in which information is consciously rehearsed, elaborated, and linked to existing knowledge. Short-term memory is said to have limited capacity and limited duration.

D1. ★Pop-Up: An Experiment in Short-Term Memory

In this activity, the goal is to examine the limits of short-term memory by testing the student's memory for repeating patterns of color.

An Experiment in Short-Term Memory

Activity Type: Simulation

Learning Objective: Learn about the limits of short-term memory.

Faculty Note: In this Simon-like activity, the goal is to examine the limits of short-term memory by testing memory for patterns of color. On each trial, the computer will present a series of lights and the student's task is to repeat the series by clicking on each color in the order that it appeared; the series gets longer as the activity progresses.

Students should notice that as the number of items in the sequence increased, their memory probably became less reliable. It is harder to hold nine items in working memory than it is to remember two items. Research suggests that most people are only able to keep between five and nine items in short-term memory at any given time.

It should be noted that this is only demonstrating the limitations of short-term (working) memory, not long-term memory.

Additional Resources:

George Miller's seminal paper on memory, *The Magical Number Seven, Plus or Minus Two: Some Limits on Our Capacity for Processing Information* can be found at http://www.well.com/user/smalin/miller.html

E. Short-Term Memory and Chunking

The amount of information that can be processed in short-term memory depends on our ability to organize the material. One way to increase our memory capacity is by "chunking" information into a smaller number of meaningful units.

E1. ★A Test of Memory IV

An exercise in organizing a string of digits into "dates" (meaningful chunks of four numbers, such as 1998) illustrates the role of organization in short-term memory.

A Test of Memory IV

Activity Type: Audio and Animated Demonstration

Learning Objective: Learn about the role that organization (i.e., chunking) can play in short-term memory.

Faculty Note: Students hear a series of numbers presented individually, and then the numbers are organized into meaningful "chunks" such as dates ("1998") to illustrate the advantages this offers in the encoding process.

It should be easy to come up with additional "chunking" demonstrations that would facilitate recall, e.g., C F B I I I A R S = FBI, CIA, IRS.

F. Long-Term Memory Storage

Long-term memory is described as a practically limitless store of information and experience that persists over long durations.

G. Long Term Memory and the Serial Position Effect

The serial position effect refers to the finding that when people attempt to remember a long list of items, they tend to remember more items from early in the list, a few items from late in the list, and relatively fewer items from the middle of the list. The concepts of short-term and long-term memory are needed to account for this finding.

H. Long-Term Memory and Depth of Processing

It is noted here that a factor that determines whether items make it into long-term memory is the "depth" of processing that is involved. The example given is of the effects of structural vs. semantic judgments on eventual recall.

I. Stage 3: Memory Retrieval

In order to say that you've "remembered" something, you have to be able to retrieve it. Many failures of memory are problems with retrieval, not encoding or storage. The "tip of the tongue" phenomenon is given as an illustration.

I1. ★Pop-Up: Types of Retrieval

A memory exercise is used to distinguish between recall memory and recognition memory. Recognition memory tends to be significantly easier because the item itself provides a retrieval cue.

Types of Retrieval

Activity Type: Demonstration

Learning Objective: Learn to distinguish between recall and recognition memory.

Faculty Note: Recall refers to the ability to reproduce an item that you've previously been exposed to. In contrast, recognition memory refers to the ability to recognize an item that you've previously been exposed to. Recognition memory tends to be significantly easier because the item itself provides a retrieval cue. Students can demonstrate this for themselves by trying to retrieve items via both recall and recognition.

J. The Construction of Memory

Although memories feel as if they are "recordings", it is more likely that they are "reconstructions." The research of Elizabeth Loftus on the unreliability of eyewitness testimony provides many examples of the discrepancy between memory and reality. The misinformation effect and the construction of false memories are discussed.

J1. ★Pop-Up: A Demonstration of Déjà Vu

The experience of déjà vu is used as a starting point to discuss inaccuracies in retrieval. Psychologists who study memory would argue that these experiences can be explained simply as a natural consequence of the way in which the mind stores and retrieves information.

A Demonstration of Déjà Vu

Activity Type: Demonstration

Learning Objective: Encourage students to question the everyday assumption that memory is a passive recording and is almost always accurate.

Faculty Note: In this demonstration, students hear a list of eighteen words that are linked by a "medical" theme (i.e., hospital, nurse, etc.). Their task is to try to remember the words without writing them down or repeating them out loud. After completing the list, they are given a recognition memory test. Many students will falsely remember that the word "doctor" appeared on the list because of its similarity to other words that were on the list. In fact, the word does not appear on the list of words to be remembered.

False alarms such as this (sometimes referred to as feelings of "déjà vu") can be explained as the result of basic memory processes.

J2. ★Pop-Up: A Demonstration in Point of View and Memory

A simple recall exercise is used here to demonstrate the constructed nature of memories and how they can diverge significantly from actual events.

A Demonstration of Point of View and Memory

Activity Type: Demonstration

Learning Objective: Encourage students to question the everyday assumptions that memory is a passive recording and that simple episodic memories are almost always accurate.

Faculty Note: Students are simply asked to remember the last occasion on which they went swimming. Some will remember swimming from the same visual perspective they had at the time of the event (i.e., from a "first-person" perspective). Many people, however, "remember"

the event as if they were spectators, outside their bodies watching themselves. In other words, they "remember" the event from a perspective they could not have had.

This may provide a vivid and personal example of the transformations which memories sometimes undergo, and of the sometimes automatic assumptions we make concerning the reliability of memories.

Rapid Review 4

Quick Quiz

Instructors' Quizzes

1. People have speculated about psychological phenomenon

   A. for only the past forty to fifty years.
   B. for approximately 120 years, since 1879.
   C. since the birth of the U.S.A.
   D. since the time of the most ancient philosophers.

2. Why is Wilhelm Wundt considered the "father" of psychology?

   A. He developed a technique of introspection to study the content of the mind.
   B. He wrote many books that are still used by contemporary psychologists.
   C. He established the first psychology laboratory and declared psychology to be a science.
   D. He applied the ideas of Aristotle toward understanding behavior.

3. The goal of structuralism was to

   A. determine the purpose of behavior.
   B. break down consciousness into its most basic elements.
   C. discover the connection between the conscious and unconscious mind.
   D. understand how the brain and nerves control behavior.

4. The goal of functionalism was to

   A. explain how behavior aids in survival and adaptation.
   B. develop scientific, laboratory-based psychology.
   C. determine the basic elements of mental experience.
   D. use pure reasoning to understand behavior.

5. According to the psychoanalytic perspective, the most powerful forces determining human behavior is (are)

   A. the brain and nervous system.
   B. the unconscious.
   C. the environment.
   D. perceptions and values.

6. Dr. Spence is interested in explaining people's behavior by looking at the past history of the human species. She is doing research in

   A. psychoanalysis.
   B. evolutionary psychology.
   C. behaviorism.
   D. gestalt psychology.

7. Science can be distinguished from other ways of knowing by

   A. its precision.

B.   its use of electricity.
C.   its use of faith and common sense.
D.   its reliance on empirical evidence.

8.   Which of the following statements most accurately describes the scientific principle of falsifiability?

A.   If any theory is tested long enough, it will be shown to be untrue.
B.   If a hypothesis is shown to be false, then the theory it is based on is also false.
C.   A truly scientific theory must have the potential to be false.
D.   For a theory to be true, there must be supporting anecdotal evidence.

9.   The purpose of naturalistic observation is to

A.   predict behavior, especially unusual behavior.
B.   describe behavior as it occurs in the environment.
C.   connect peoples' current behavior with their early experiences.
D.   explain why certain behaviors occur repeatedly.

10.   Which of the following correlations is the strongest?

A.   +.67
B.   −.81
C.   +.01
D.   −.15

11.   The behavior that the researcher tries to predict is called the

A.   dependent variable.
B.   observation.
C.   independent variable.
D.   control variable.

12.   If caffeine consumption is correlated with anxiety, we know that caffeine causes anxiety.

A.   true
B.   false

13.   The hindsight bias is the tendency to

A.   overestimate the predictability of a past event.
B.   underestimate the predictability of a past event.
C.   see things in a rearview mirror more clearly.

14. In a repeated measures design, each subject

A.   is randomly assigned to one of the conditions.
B.   is measured before and after the treatment.
C.   is measured a minimum of three times.
D.   is assumed to be representative of the general population.

15. The Cardassians wanted to test Captain Picard's tolerance for pain. They hooked him up to an electric shock generator and measured the decibel level of his screams as a function of shock voltage. The Cardassians were interested in developing a technique for use in extracting Federation secrets. The independent variable in this experiment is the _____ and the dependent variable is the _____

A.   intensity of the shock voltage; loudness of the scream.
B.   tolerance for pain; loudness of the scream.
C.   loudness of the scream; intensity of the shock voltage.
D.   intensity of the shock voltage; federation secrets.

1. Why is Wilhelm Wundt considered the "father" of psychology?

   A. He developed the technique of introspection to study the contents of the mind.
   B. He wrote many books that are still used by contemporary psychologists.
   C. He established the first psychology laboratory and declared psychology to be a science.
   D. He applied the ideas of Descartes toward understanding behavior.

2. The goal of functionalism was to

   A. explain how behavior aids in survival and adaptation.
   B. develop a scientific laboratory-based psychology.
   C. determine the basic elements of mental experience.
   D. use pure reasoning to understand behavior.

3. According to Freud, conscious forces have more power over behavior than unconscious forces do.

   A. true
   B. false

4. A(n) _____ is a detailed description of a single individual or group.

   A. correlational study
   B. survey
   C. case study
   D. experiment

4. If a researcher wants to determine empirically whether there is a relationship between learning to play sports at an early age and the ability to do well in high school, which method would be most appropriate to use?

   A. case study
   B. correlational
   C. naturalistic observation
   D. laboratory observation

6. If the correlation between height and shoe size is found to be _____, then a very tall woman would be expected to have a very small shoe size.

   A. +.92
   B. +.33
   C. -.18
   D. -.87

7. Which of these methods is best suited for determining cause-effect relationships?
A. experimentation
B. laboratory observation
C. naturalistic observation
D. case study

8. This technique is used in order to create groups in an experiment that are as equal as possible in terms of history, education, experience, health, etc., prior to the beginning of the experiment.

A. random assignment
B. single blind
C. representative sampling
D. rotational analysis

9. A correlational study that found a high positive correlation between the attractiveness of the salesperson and our desire to buy a product would allow us to conclude that it is the attractiveness of the salesperson which causes our increased desire to buy the product.

A. true
B. false

10. The goal of humanistic psychology is to

A. understand the social context in which human behavior occurs.
B. aid individuals in expressing themselves and reaching their full human potential.
C. make conscious the unconscious forces that determine human behavior and mental processes.
D. understand the mental processes that are specific to human beings, such as language, imagination, problem solving, etc.

1. A psychologist predicts that entering students with higher SAT or ACT scores will have higher GPAs all through college. This is a(n)

    A. theory.
    B. hypothesis.
    C. confirmation
    D. principle.

2. A researcher finds a negative correlation between annual family income and rates of infant death. In other words,

    A. lower incomes are associated with higher rates of infant death.
    B. a low income causes parents to neglect their newborn infants.
    C. higher income parents love and care for their infants more consistently and carefully.
    D. lower income families tend to have more children.

3. Introspection

    A. became the dominant method in current-day psychology.
    B. came to be known as functionalism.
    C. involved carefully analyzing and observing your own mental experiences under controlled condition.
    D. helped psychologists identify personality characteristics in people by reading bumps on their heads.

4. The goal of structuralism was to

    A. develop a structure from which psychology could preceed.
    B. analyze experience (i.e., sensations, images, feelings) into its basic elements.
    C. identify the function and purpose of behavior.
    D. discover the structural basis of behavior.

5. Behaviorism emphasizes the observation and measurement of overt acts and reactions.

    A. true
    B. false

6. When using this method, psychologists systematically observe and record behaviors without interfering in any way with the organism being observed.

    A. experimental method
    B. survey method
    C. psychological test
    D. observational method

7. If there is a positive correlation between anxiety and score achieved on a test, then a person with high anxiety would be likely to

A. score high on the test
B. score low on the test
C. score zero on the test
D. be unable to complete the test

8. Which of the following correlations would allow a researcher to make the most accurate prediction or estimate of one factor if the value of the other factor were known?

A. −.22
B. −.98
C. +.46
D. +.83

9. The factor which is manipulated by the experimenter is called the _____ variable.

A. controlled
B. dependent
C. independent
D. intervening

10. An experimenter wants to determine whether workers produce more widgets under bright light or under subdued lighting conditions. In this experiment, the independent variable will be the number of widgets produced.

A. true
B. false

1.	The current view of the field of psychology is that

A.	almost all development is strictly determined by inherited characteristics.
B.	all that a person becomes is due to the environment in which he or she develops.
C.	heredity and environment interact to produce both psychological and physical traits.

2.	The basic units of the nervous system are

A.	neurons.
B.	lobes.
C.	axons.
D.	genes.

3.	Which part of a neuron transmits data to other neurons, or muscle or gland cells?

A.	the dendrites
B.	the soma
C.	the axon
D.	the glial cells

4.	When we talk about neurons, the "all or none" principle refers to the

A.	rule that before a neuron will fire, all of the necessary neurotransmitters must be present.
B.	common reflex that makes you kick your whole leg, not part of it.
C.	neuron getting all the rest it needs before firing again.
D.	neuron always firing at full strength if there is enough excitation.

5.	The medulla and pons are part of the

A.	cerebral cortex.
B.	hind brain.
C.	limbic system.
D.	cerebellum.

6.	The brain structure that contributes the most to balance and muscular coordination is the

A.	cerebellum
B.	corpus callosum
C.	medulla
D.	hypothalamus

7. If you suffered a brain injury and now have difficulty controlling the left side of your body, which half of the brain was probably injured?

A.   east
B.   west
C.   right
D.   left

8. If we are "prepared" by our evolutionary heritage to learn to be afraid of snakes, this would be an example of a _____ cause of behavior.

A.   distal
B.   proximal

9. The division of the nervous system which contains the brain and spinal cord is the

A.   central nervous system.
B.   peripheral nervous system.
C.   sensory nervous system.
D.   motor nervous system.

10. Because it seems that there are always wars being fought somewhere in the world, it is tempting to assume that aggression and violence are an essential and even normal part of human nature. This reasoning might be an example of

A.   the deterministic fallacy.
B.   the naturalistic fallacy.
C.   the positivistic fallacy.
D.   the nominal fallacy.

11. Which of the following is not an assumption of the theory of natural selection?

A.   individuals differ from one another in many ways
B.   some traits can be inherited
C.   some traits make reproductive success more likely
D.   individuals must be aggressive to survive

12. Broca's area and Wernicke's area in the brain appear to be involved in

A.   language.
B.   pain perception.
C.   vision.
D.   muscle coordination.

13. The case of Phineas Gage was instructive because it illustrated

A. that brain damage is always fatal
B. that brain damage can affect personality traits
C. that individuals can function normally after extensive brain damage
D. that the frontal lobes are responsible for balance and coordination.

14. The structure that allows extensive communication between the hemispheres of the brain is the

A. hypothalamus
B. occipital lobe
C. corpus callosum
D. vesicle

15. The sum of all of the excitatory and inhibitory influences on the neuron is called the:

A. action potential
B. resting potential
C. potent potential
D. graded potential

Biopsychology Instructor's Quiz One

1.   The principle of natural selection was first formulated by

A.   Thorndike.
B.   Mendel.
C.   Freud.
D.   Darwin.

2.   The two major divisions of the nervous system are the _____ nervous systems.

A.   primary and secondary
B.   sympathetic and parasympathetic
C.   somatic and autonomic
D.   central and peripheral

3.   The _____ nervous system controls voluntary action.

A.   somatic
B.   autonomic
C.   sympathetic
D.   parasympathetic

4.   The sympathetic and parasympathetic nerves are divisions of the _____ nervous system.

A.   central
B.   somatic
C.   voluntary
D.   autonomic

5.   The primary function of this part of a neuron is to keep the cell alive.

A.   axon
B.   cell body
C.   dendrite
D.   myelin sheath

6.   Impulses which travel from one neuron to another must cross the

A.   blood-brain barrier
B.   synaptic cleft
C.   axonic junction
D.   somatic membrane

7.   Neurotransmitters are stored in the

A.   synaptic cleft.
B.   fatty tissue of the myelin sheath.

C. cell body.

D. vesicles in the axon terminals.

8. At an excitatory synapse,

A. there is a voltage shift in the positive direction.

B. the receiving neuron becomes less likely to fire.

C. the cell membrane becomes less permeable to positive ions.

D. re-uptake is prevented.

9. The cerebral hemispheres are connected by the _____.

A. amygdala

B. medulla

C. olfactory bulb

D. corpus callosum

10. Broca's area and Wernicke's area are known to be involved in

A. music

B. planning

C. decision making

D. language

Biopsychology: Instructor's Quiz Two

1.   The area which controls body sensations is located in this part of the cortex.

A.   temporal
B.   occipital
C.   frontal
D.   parietal

2.   The _____ nervous system contains the brain and spinal cord.

A.   central
B.   peripheral
C.   sympathetic
D.   autonomic

3.   Which of these is most likely to be controlled by the autonomic nervous system?

A.   the amount of blood flow through the kidneys
B.   playing the piano
C.   memorizing a poem
D.   riding a bicycle

4.   The _____ nervous system prepares the body for flight or fight in times of stress.

A.   parasympathetic
B.   sympathetic
C.   central
D.   somatic

5.   This part of the neuron acts as a receiver, picking up information from other cells.

A.   axon
B.   cell body
C.   dendrite
D.   myelin sheath

6.   The action potential is due to

A.   the presence of hormones on the axonic membrane.
B.   the flow of sodium and potassium ions across the axonic membrane.
C.   an electrical "short circuiting" of the myelin sheath.
D.   too great a space between the axon and the myelin sheath.

7.   At an inhibitory synapse,

A.   there is a voltage shift in the positive direction.
B.   the receiving neuron becomes less likely to fire.

C.   information converges from exactly three sources.
D.   all of these are true

8.   Endorphins

A.   reduce pain.
B.   increase sensory sensitivity.
C.   speed up learning.
D.   improve memory.

9.   Damage to the cerebellum might interfere with which of the following?

A.   musical memory
B.   balance
C.   breathing
D.   vision

10.   The fact that the left hemisphere and right hemisphere of the cerebral cortex have
      somewhat different functions is referred to as

A.   localization.
B.   lateralization.
C.   redundancy reduction.
D.   articulation.

1. The organization and interpretation of incoming sensory data is called

A. sensation.
B. attention.
C. perception.
D. psychophysics.

2. We are able to distinguish the sound of a cello from that of a violin because of the process of

A. feature detection.
B. attention.
C. sensory coding.
D. signal detection.

3. In a darkened room, if one candle is added to two candles already on the birthday cake, the change is very noticeable. In an equally dark room, when one candle is added to forty-nine candles already on the birthday cake, little change in brightness is noticed. This is a problem in

A. transduction.
B. signal detection.
C. perceptual constancy.
D. psychophysics.

4. The smallest amount of energy that a person can detect reliably is known as what kind of threshold?

A. absolute
B. difference
C. perceptual
D. decision

5. A friend who is a heavy smoker invites you to his apartment. When you first enter, you are repulsed by the strong odor of stale smoke. After several minutes, you no longer are aware of the smell. What has occurred?

A. signal detection
B. sensory overload
C. feature detection
D. sensory adaptation

6. The wavelengths of light give us our experience of

A. color.
B. brightness.

C.   saturation.
D.   complexity.

7.   An eyewitness sees a suspect run through the dark woods. When questioned, the witness states she could clearly see that the suspect was wearing a baseball cap but could not tell its color. This is because

A.   the iris constricts the size of the pupil and less light enters the eye.
B.   the image of the suspect is upside down on the retina.
C.   the fovea enlarges in darkness, and therefore shapes but not colors can be perceived.
D.   cones require a higher level of light stimulation compared to rods.

8.   Feature detectors are

A.   bundles of the axons of the ganglion cells which form the optic nerve.
B.   specialized cells in the brain that respond to particular forms such as lines or angles
C.   qualities in the rods and cones that respond to dim light or color, respectively.
D.   stimuli just above threshold levels that often are undetected by the eye.

9.   What structure in the ear has the same function as the rod and cones of the retina?

A.   the three bones of the middle ear
B.   the eardrum
C.   the cilia
D.   the cochlea

10.   Researchers agree that the four basic taste sensations are

A.   sweet, salty, bitter and strong.
B.   salty, sour, bitter and sweet.
C.   acidic, tart, sweet and salty.
D.   sweet, sharp, salty and fishy.

11.   Psychologists who are interested in relating how the physical properties of a stimulus are relate to the psychological experience of that stimulus are called

A.   gestalt psychologists.
B.   psychophysicists.
C.   biopsychologists.
D.   parapsychologists.

12. To save costs, the executives at a large cola manufacturer want to cut down on the amount of sweetener that is in their product. At the same time, their product is very successful and they don't want the taste to change. These executives are confronted with a problem involving

A. absolute threshold.
B. sensory adaptation.
C. difference threshold.
D. sensory transduction.

1. The receiving of physical energy as input from the environment and the changing of this energy into nervous system activity is

A. activation.
B. transduction.
C. perception.
D. recognition.

2. Spending time in the dark results in the visual receptors

A. becoming more sensitive to light.
B. becoming less sensitive to light.
C. not responding to light stimuli at all.
D. responding to light about the same as before.

3. In light stimuli, wavelength determines

A. intensity.
B. amplitude.
C. color.
D. brightness.

4. The part of the eye where vision is most acute is the

A. fovea.
B. iris.
C. cornea.
D. retina.

5. Luis dropped a quarter in the movie theater. Since it is quite dark in there, the part(s) of his eye that will help him most in finding the lost coin is/are his

A. cones.
B. rods.
C. lens.
D. cornea.

6. Complementary afterimages provide support for the

A. trichromatic theory.
B. signal detection theory.
C. effects of subliminal stimuli.
D. opponent-process theory.

7. A pure light made up of wavelengths that are all the same length would be

A. red.
B. white.
C. invisible.
D. monochromatic.

8. The psychological experience associated with a light's wavelength is

A. color.
B. brightness.
C. amplitude.
D. intensity.

9. The process in which the ciliary muscles change the shape of the lens is called

A. adaptation.
B. accommodation.
C. sensing.
D. transduction.

10. Motion afterimages appear to be the result of adaptation occurring in

A. the retina.
B. the brain.
C. the rods.
D. the cones.

Sensation: Instructor's Quiz Two

1. Manuella enjoys the wonderful smells from the kitchen when she first arrives at her mother's house, but after a while, she no longer notices them. What accounts for this?

    A. sensory adaptation
    B. selective attention
    C. absolute thresholds
    D. difference thresholds

2. Humans experience the wavelength of light as

    A. hue or color.
    B. brightness.
    C. deepness.
    D. complexity.

3. The fovea contains

    A. only rods.
    B. only cones.
    C. an equal number of rods and cones.
    D. more rods than cones.

4. The visual receptors are located in the

    A. cornea.
    B. pupil.
    C. lens.
    D. retina.

5. Which theory of color vision best explains negative afterimages?

    A. trichromatic theory
    B. opponent-process theory
    C. doctrine of specific nerve energies
    D. Weber's law

6. Pitch is the dimension of sound related to the

    A. amplitude of a pressure wave.
    B. frequency of a pressure wave.
    C. distinguishing quality of a sound.
    D. complexity of a pressure wave.

7. The part of the ear that plays the same role in hearing as the retina plays in vision is called the

A. cochlea.
B. eardrum.
C. organ of Corti.
D. auditory nerve.

8. Scientists agree that humans have only five senses.

A. true
B. false

9. A cost-conscious soft drink manufacturer wants to determine how little sweetener he can add to a new soft drink and still have consumers think of the drink as tasting "sweet". This is a problem involving

A. absolute thresholds.
B. difference thresholds.
C. adaptation.
D. the occipital cortex.

10. The field of research that is concerned with how physical events are related to our psychological experience of them is called

A. psychoanalysis.
B. psychophysics.
C. signal detection.
D. physiological psychology.

Ear Structure Labeling Activity
Ear Function Labeling Activity

Perception: CD-ROM Quick Quiz

1. According to signal detection theory, response bias influences

   A. a decision process.
   B. a sensory process.
   C. both decision and sensory processes.
   D. neither decision nor sensory processes.

2. Mark sees four people sitting together in class on the first day and assumes they know each other even though, at the moment, they are not even talking to each other. Mark's judgment may be influenced by the Gestalt principle of

   A. closure.
   B. figure-ground.
   C. proximity.
   D. similarity.

3. Which of the following is a binocular depth cue?

   A. interposition
   B. linear perspective
   C. relative size
   D. retinal disparity

4. The retinal image of your pet dog is getting larger and larger. You perception is that the dog is running toward you, NOT that the dog is actually getting larger. The perceptual principle at work here is

   A. size constancy.
   B. convergence.
   C. shape constancy.
   D. linear perspective.

5. One of the major reasons that psychologists find visual illusions interesting is because they

   A. are opportunities for our subconscious desires to reveal themselves in our waking experience.
   B. prove to us all that we are still human and less than perfect, so we don't overrate our self-esteem.
   C. give our perceptual system practice so we will be better prepared for the unpredictable future.
   D. highlight predictable errors we make in perception that provide hints about our perceptual strategies.

6.   The phi phenomenon is

A.   the tendency to see motion in a series of static images presented at the correct rate.
B.   the tendency of sound to dissipate at a constant rate.
C.   the tendency for retinal disparity to increase as objects get closer.
D.   the tendency of physicians to raise their rates proportional to the rate of inflation.

7.   Bottom-up illusions tend to be very compelling because they

A.   are learned early in life.
B.   tend to be hard wired.
C.   are socially constructed.
D.   involve expectations on the part of the perceiver.

8.   As you gaze at a sunrise over the mountains, your brain combines many different elements of information to create a single, unified impression. This organization and impression is called

A.   feature detection.
B.   depth cue analysis.
C.   sensation.
D.   perception.

9.   The difference between how an object is seen by each eye is called

A.   retinal disparity.
B.   linear perspective.
C.   interposition.
D.   convergence.

10.   During the summer, Meghan and Michael eagerly wait for the ice cream truck. It typically comes down the street at 5 p.m. As the afternoon progresses, they repeatedly run to the front door, convinced that they heard the ice cream truck. Their behavior is best explained by

A.   the principle of sensory adaptation.
B.   difference thresholds.
C.   signal detection theory.
D.   acoustic illusions.

1. According to signal detection theory, experiencing a stimulus is a matter of

A. decision-making.
B. detectability of the stimulus.
C. response bias.
D. all of the above.
E. none of the above.

2. Retinal disparity is to binocular cue as _____ is to monocular cue.

A. convergence
B. size constancy
C. texture
D. continuity

3. Which of the following is NOT a pictorial depth cue?

A. dark adaptation
B. linear perspective
C. relative size
D. interposition

4. As Dorothy traveled down the "yellow brick road," if she looked down at her feet, the bricks would appear their normal size. However, if she looked ahead down the road, the bricks would appear to be smaller. This can be explained by the perceptual phenomenon of

A. linear perspective.
B. texture gradient.
C. interposition.
D. relative size.

5. A person who has lived all his life in the dense jungle and thus has not perceived any stimulus from a great distance would most likely NOT have developed

A. shape constancy.
B. light constancy.
C. size constancy.
D. all of the above.
E. none of the above.

6. The Hermann Grid is an example of

A. a top-down illusion.
B. a bottom-up illusion.
C. a left-right illusion.
D. a depth cue.

7. The Twisted Cords Illusion is an example of

A. a top-down illusion.
B. a bottom-up illusion.
C. a left-right illusion.
D. a depth cue..

8. To reach an absolute threshold, stimuli must be detected at least fifty percent of the time.

A. true
B. false

9. Sensation and perception are essentially the same thing.

A. true
B. false

10. Closure and proximity are examples of Gestalt principles in perception.

A. true
B. false

Perception Instructor's Quiz Two

1. Signal detection theory takes into account

    A. observers' response biases.
    B. sensory differences among species.
    C. the role of feature detectors.
    D. which cells are firing, how many cells are firing and the rate at which they fire.

2. Which Gestalt strategy would explain why you see $$$AAA### as three groups of figures instead of nine separate figures?

    A. closure
    B. figure-ground
    C. continuity
    D. similarity

3. The slight difference in sideways separation between two objects as seen by the left eye and the right eye is called

    A. a binocular cue.
    B. a depth cue.
    C. retinal disparity.
    D. all of the above

4. As you watch a door opening, its image changes from rectangular to trapezoidal, yet you continue to think of the door as rectangular. What explains this phenomenon?

    A. perceptual constancy
    B. retinal disparity
    C. monocular depth cues
    D. selective attention

5. Perception differs from sensation in that

    A. perception allows us to organize and interpret sensations.
    B. perception is the raw data coming in from the senses.
    C. sensation is an organizing and interpretive process, perception is not.
    D. perception can be measured, sensations cannot.

6. At the art museum, you look at what appears to be a canvas covered with millions of brightly colored dots. As you continue looking, you suddenly see that it is a picture of a vase filled with brightly colored flowers. What has happened?

A. The light that is entering your eye has changed.
B. Adaptation has occurred and you have become more sensitive to the colors in the picture.
C. Your brain has organized and interpreted the sensations as familiar forms.
D. The light waves reflecting from the picture have shifted so that they are now above your absolute threshold.

7. When we listen to someone speaking to us, we may only hear between 60 and 80 percent of what they are saying, but we usually understand the meaning of what has been said. Which Gestalt principle might be used to explain this phenomenon?

A. closure
B. figure-ground
C. proximity
D. similarity

8. As you look across a field, you see an apple tree that is obscuring your view of a farm house. You assume that the tree is closer to you than the farm house. This perception is based on the depth cue known as

A. interposition.
B. convergence.
C. proximity.
D. linear perspective.

9. Most illusions occur because the stimulus actually changes.

A. true
B. false

10. In signal detection terms, when a person says that a stimulus is present but it's actually not there, it is called a

A. hit.
B. miss.
C. correct rejection.
D. false alarm.

1.   Learning can be observed in

A.   primates.
B.   humans.
C.   vertebrates.
D.   any organism with a nervous system.

2.   Maria blinks when a puff of air is blown into her eyes. In classical conditioning, the blink is considered to be a/an

A.   unconditioned response.
B.   learned response.
C.   neutral response.
D.   conditioned response.

3.   Chuck has learned that if a toilet is flushed while he is taking a shower, he will immediately be scalded by very hot water. His response to this unpleasant stimulus is to jump out of the way. After a few times of this, Chuck jumps as soon as he hears the sound of the toilet flushing. In this example of classical conditioning, the hot water is the _____ and the sound of the toilet flushing is the _____.

A.   unconditioned stimulus; conditioned stimulus
B.   neutral stimulus; conditioned stimulus
C.   earned stimulus; neutral stimulus
D.   unconditioned stimulus; unconditioned response

4.   Paul has always had a grand time every St. Patrick's day. As a result, whenever he sees a shamrock, he smiles. This is an example of

A.   aversive conditioning.
B.   instrumental conditioning.
C.   operant conditioning.
D.   classical conditioning.

5.   In John Watson's studies with Little Albert, after the classical conditioning procedure the rat had become the

A.   neutral stimulus.
B.   generalized stimulus
C.   unconditioned stimulus.
D.   conditioned stimulus.

6.   One problem with John Watson's research involving Little Albert is that

A.   the conclusions were misinterpreted.
B.   Little Albert was an atypical subject.

C.   the research was interrupted and never completed.

D.   by today's standards, the research was unethical.

7.   Which statement best characterizes the "law of effect?"

A.   In the proper setting, learning can override heredity.

B.   Good things tend to happen to good people.

C.   Behaviors are influenced by their consequences.

D.   Behavioral change follows most readily from cognitive change.

8.   A fundamental difference between classical and operant conditioning is that

A.   in operant conditioning, the desired response has to occur before it can be reinforced.

B.   in classical conditioning, responses are not reinforced.

C.   in operant conditioning there is no stimulus generalization.

D.   in classical conditioning, extinguished responses do not spontaneously recover.

9.   What is the difference between positive reinforcement and negative reinforcement?

A.   Positive reinforcement is classically conditioned and negative reinforcement is operantly conditioned.

B.   Positive reinforcement increases the probability of a response and negative reinforcement decreases the probability of a response.

C.   Positive reinforcement uses primary reinforcers and negative reinforcement uses secondary reinforcers.

D.   A stimulus is presented after a response in positive reinforcement and a stimulus is removed in negative reinforcement.

10.   Which of the following was difficult for so-called "radical" behaviorists to explain?

A.   positive reinforcement

B.   the law of effect

C.   trial and error learning

D.   language development

11.   _____ is (are) an example of a primary reinforcer.

A.   grades

B.   money

C.   water

D.   praise

12.   The pioneering researcher Hermann Ebbinghaus studied memory for

A.   nonsense syllables.

B.   faces.

C.   names.

D.   household objects.

13.   Once information is in memory, we must keep it there. This process is called

A.   retrieval.
B.   storage.
C.   perception.
D.   encoding.

14.   All information that eventually gets stored in our memories must first enter our _____
      memory.

A.   sensory
B.   episodic
C.   semantic
D.   short-term

15.   The type of memory with large capacity and very long duration is

A.   sensory memory.
B.   short-term memory.
C.   long-term memory.
D.   procedural memory.

16.   The capacity of short-term memory can be increased through

A.   chunking.
B.   recognition.
C.   rehearsal.
D.   selective attention.

17.   In order to get information into short-term memory, we must at least

A.   chunk the information.
B.   pay attention to the information.
C.   know what the information means.
D.   engage in elaborative rehearsal.

18.   Memory appears to function as if it is _____ actual events.

A.   a reconstruction of
B.   a taped replay of
C.   completely unrelated to
D.   all of the above

19. A professor who wants to measure her students' recognition memory should give them a(an) _____ test.

A. multiple choice
B. essay
C. short answer
D. fill-in-the-blanks

20. For which of the following methods are individuals provided with the fewest possible cues to aid retrieval?

A. metamemory
B. recall
C. method of loci
D. recognition

1. Four-year-old John has used the word "ran" correctly in the past. Now he says "I runned home." This is a sign of

   A. overregularization.
   B. retardation.
   C. a learning disability.
   D. psycholinguistic underdevelopment.

2. This physiologist originated the study of classical conditioning.

   A. Skinner
   B. Bandura
   C. Pavlov
   D. Thorndike

3. In classical conditioning, the _____ stimulus elicits a response automatically or reflexively, even without training.

   A. respondent
   B. conditioned
   C. discriminative
   D. unconditioned

4. If a consequence strengthens a response, that consequence can be considered to be

   A. neutral
   B a punisher.
   C. a reinforcer.
   D a biologically based.

5. In a laboratory, a loud noise sounds and continues until a rat presses a bar. Over time, the rat presses the bar more and more. The abatement of the loud noise is functioning as a

   A. positive reinforcer
   B. negative reinforcer
   C. positive punisher
   D. negative punisher

6. Reinforcer is to punisher as

   A. positive is to negative
   B. strong is to weak
   C. primary is to secondary
   D. increased responding is to decreased responding

7.   When every correct response that an organism makes is reinforced, this schedule of reinforcement is in effect.

A.   fixed interval
B.   continuous
C.   variable ratio
D.   variable interval

8.   Taste aversions are probably learned through a process of classical conditioning.

A.   true
B.   false

9.   Money, praise, and applause are examples of common secondary reinforcers.

A.   true
B.   false

10.   The type of memory tested in games like Jeopardy or Trivial Pursuit is

A.   relearning
B.   recognition
C.   recall
D.   priming

11.   In _____, information is retained for a second or two, before it is passed on for further processing.

A.   short-term memory
B.   long-term memory
C.   sensory memory
D.   distributed memory

12.   Based on the classic forgetting curve of Ebbinghaus, if you had to predict how the forgetting of non-meaningful material is likely to proceed, you would predict that

A.   very little forgetting would occur until at least three days had passed, at which point forgetting would start to increase rapidly.
B.   most of the forgetting would occur within a few hours, and then forgetting would taper off.
C.   forgetting would occur in a constant linear fashion until it reached 100% after five days.
D.   no forgetting would occur until at least a week had passed, and then forgetting would increase very gradually.

13.   Memory research indicates that memory is like a video camera, recording every moment of one's life.

A.   true

B. false

14. If you are trying to remember a long grocery list, you are more likely to remember the middle items than the items at the end of the list.

A. true
B. false

15. Unless there is a conscious effort to hold the information longer, after about 30 seconds information has disappeared from

A. sensory memory
B. short-term memory
C. long-term memory
D. implicit memory

Learning and Memory: Instructor's Quiz Two

1. What is the difference between the behaviorist and cognitive explanations of learning?

A. Behaviorists emphasize past events and cognitive psychologists emphasize potential events?
B. Behaviorists emphasize potential events and cognitive psychologists emphasize past events.
C. Behaviorists emphasize mental explanations while cognitive psychologists emphasize the reinforcement history of the organism.
D. Behaviorists emphasize the reinforcement history of the organism while cognitive psychologists emphasize mental explanations.

2. Any response that decreases responding is a negative reinforcer.

A. true
B. false

3. Maggie ate some tainted fish during a train ride and became sick. Now, whenever she is on a moving train, she feels nauseated. In this example, the sensation of the moving train serves as the

A. unconditioned stimulus
B. unconditioned response
C. conditioned response
D. conditioned stimulus

4. Drug addicts are at greater risk for overdosing if they take the same amount of a drug as they usually take

A. in a strange environment.
B. but wait longer after the previous administration than usual before taking the drug again.
C. in the same environment as they usually are in when they take it.
D. with no one else present.

5. Any consequence of a response which weakens the response is

A. punishment.
B. biologically based.
C. neutral.
D. reinforcement.

6. Which of the following is an example of negative reinforcement?

A. a teenager uses bad language to get attention from friends
B. a child has a temper tantrum in order to induce her parents to buy her a toy
C. a man reads a mystery novel for fun
D. a woman smokes a cigarette because it reduces jittery, anxious feelings.

7. In this schedule of reinforcement, reinforcers are delivered only after a set number of responses has been completed.

A. variable interval
B. variable ratio
C. fixed interval
D. fixed ratio

8. Superstition can be understood within the context of operant conditioning by realizing that the reinforcement is

A. coincidental
B. continuous
C. generalized
D. partial

9. In Pavlov's original experiment (conditioning salivary responses in dogs), the unconditioned stimulus was meat powder.

A. true
B. false

10. Multiple choice exams test which measure of memory?

A. recall
B. recognition
C. relearning
D. implicit memory

11. _____ has unlimited capacity.

A. short-term memory
B. sensory memory
C. long-term memory
D. distributed memory

12. In order to use it, information that has been entered into memory has to be recovered as some later time. The recovery of information that is already in memory is called

A. retrieval
B. encoding
C. storage
D. long-term potentiation

13. Which of the following is true of sensory memory?

A. sensory memory only exists for information that is presented visually.
B. Information from sensory memory that does not get transferred to short-term memory is lost forever.
C. Information does not enter sensory memory until it has gone through an extensive process of pattern recognition.
D. Sensory memory results in everything that is detected by our senses being stored in long-term memory.

14. The fact that the retention of any particular item in a list depends on that item's position in the list is known as the

A. short-term memory effect
B. consolidation effect
C. serial position effect
D. whole list effect

15. Our memory of past events can be influenced by the way we are asked about them

A. true
B. false

Answer Key

History and Method: CD-ROM Quick Quiz

1.	D	2.	C	3.	B
4.	A	5.	B	6.	B
7.	D	8.	C	9.	B
10.	B	11.	A	12.	B
13.	A	14.	B	15.	A

History and Method: Instructor's Quiz One

1.	C	2.	A	3.	B
4.	C	5.	B	6.	D
7.	A	8.	A	9.	B
10.	B				

History and Method: Instructor's Quiz Two

1.	B	2.	A	3.	C
4.	B	5.	A	6.	D
7.	A	8.	B	9.	C
10.	B				

Biopsychology: CD-ROM Quick Quiz

1.	C	2.	A	3.	C
4.	D	5.	B	6.	A
7.	C	8.	B	9.	A
10.	B	11.	D	12.	A
13.	B	14.	C	15.	D

Biopsychology: Instructor's Quiz One

1.	D	2.	D	3.	A
4.	D	5.	B	6.	B
7.	D	8.	A	9.	D
10.	D				

Biopsychology: Instructor's Quiz Two

1.	D	2.	A	3.	A
4.	B	5.	C	6.	B
7.	B	8.	A	9.	B
10.	B				

Sensation: CD-ROM Quick Quiz

1.	C	2.	C	3.	D
4.	A	5.	D	6.	A
7.	D	8.	B	9.	C
10.	B	11.	B	12.	C

Sensation: Instructor's Quiz One

1.	B	2.	A	3.	C
4.	A	5.	B	6.	D
7.	B	8.	A	9.	B
10.	B				

Sensation: Instructor's Quiz Two

1.	A	2.	A	3.	B
4.	D	5.	B	6.	B
7.	A	8.	B	9.	A
10.	B				

Perception: CD-ROM Quick Quiz

1.	A	2.	C	3.	D
4.	A	5.	D	6.	A
7.	B	8.	D	9.	A
10.	C				

Perception: Instructor's Quiz One

1.	D	2.	C	3.	A
4.	B	5.	C	6.	B
7.	B	8.	A	9.	B
10.	A				

Perception: Instructor's Quiz Two

1.	A	2.	D	3.	C
4.	A	5.	A	6.	C
7.	A	8.	A	9.	B
10.	D				

Learning and Memory: CD-ROM Quiz

1.	D	2.	A	3.	A
4.	D	5.	D	6.	D
7.	C	8.	A	9.	D
10.	D	11.	C	12.	A
13.	B	14.	A	15.	C
16.	A	17.	B	18.	A
19.	A	20.	B		

Learning and Memory: Instructor's Quiz One

1.	A	2.	C	3.	D
4.	C	5.	B	6.	D
7.	B	8.	A	9.	A
10.	C	11.	C	12.	B
13.	B	14.	B	15.	B

Learning and Memory: Instructor's Quiz Two

1.	D	2.	B	3.	D
4.	A	5.	A	6.	D
7.	D	8.	A	9.	A
10.	B	11.	C	12.	A
13.	B	14.	C	15.	A